ECONOMIC & PHILOSOPHIC MANUSCRIPTS OF 1844

By KARL MARX

A Digireads.com Book
Digireads.com Publishing

Economic & Philosophic Manuscripts of 1844
By Karl Marx
ISBN 10: 1-4209-5017-7
ISBN 13: 978-1-4209-5017-5

Please visit *www.digireads.com*

CONTENTS

ECONOMIC & PHILOSOPHIC MANUSCRIPTS OF 1844

PREFACE..5

WAGES OF LABOUR...8

PROFIT OF CAPITAL...16
    1. Capital...16
    2. The Profit of Capital...17
    3. The Rule of Capital over Labour and the Motives of the Capitalist 19
    4. The Accumulation of Capitals and the Competition among the Capitalists ...20

RENT OF LAND..26

ESTRANGED LABOUR 35

[ANTITHESIS OF CAPITAL AND LABOUR. LANDED PROPERTY AND
    CAPITAL]..44

[PRIVATE PROPERTY AND LABOUR. POLITICAL ECONOMY AS A
    PRODUCT OF THE MOVEMENT OF PRIVATE PROPERTY] 48

[PRIVATE PROPERTY AND COMMUNISM. VARIOUS STAGES OF
    DEVELOPMENT OF COMMUNIST VIEWS. CRUDE,
    EQUALITARIAN COMMUNISM AND COMMUNISM AS
    SOCIALISM COINCIDING WITH HUMANENESS] 50

[THE MEANING OF HUMAN REQUIREMENTSS WHERE THERE IS
    PRIVATE PROPERTY AND UNDER SOCIALISM. THE
    DIFFERENCE BETWEEN EXTRAVAGANT WEALTH AND
    INDUSTRIAL WEALTH. DIVISION OF LABOUR IN BOURGEOIS
    SOCIETY]...59

[THE POWER OF MONEY IN BOURGEOIS SOCIETY]..............................70

[CRITIQUE OF THE HEGELIAN DIALECTIC AND PHILOSOPHY AS A
    WHOLE] 73

APPENDIX

OUTLINES OF A CRITIQUE OF POLITICAL ECONOMY................................88

ECONOMIC & PHILOSOPHIC MANUSCRIPTS OF 1844[1]

PREFACE

I have already announced in the *Deutsch-Französische Jahrbücher* the critique of jurisprudence and political science in the form of a critique of the *Hegelian* philosophy of law. While preparing it for publication, the intermingling of criticism directed only against speculation with criticism of the various subjects themselves proved utterly unsuitable, hampering the development of the argument and rendering comprehension difficult. Moreover, the wealth and diversity of the subjects to be treated could have been compressed into one work only in a purely aphoristic style; whilst an aphoristic presentation of this kind, for its part, would have given the *impression* of arbitrary systematism. I shall therefore publish the critique of law, ethics, politics, etc., in a series of distinct, independent pamphlets, and afterwards try in a special work to present them again as a connected whole showing the interrelationship of the separate parts, and lastly

---

[1] The *Economic and Philosophic Manuscripts of 1844* is the first work in which Marx tried to systematically elaborate problems of political economy from the standpoint of his maturing dialectical-materialist and communist views and also to synthesise the results of his critical review of prevailing philosophic and economic theories. Apparently, Marx began to write it in order to clarify the problems for himself. But in the process of working on it he conceived the idea of publishing a work analysing the economic system of bourgeois society in his time and its ideological trends. Towards the end of his stay in Paris, on February 1, 1845, Marx signed a contract with Carl Leske, a Darmstadt publisher, concerning the publication of his work entitled *A Critique of Politics and of Political Economy*. It was to be based on his *Economic and Philosophic Manuscripts of 1844* and perhaps also on his earlier manuscript *Contribution to the Critique of Hegel's Philosophy of Law*. This plan did not materialise in the 1840s because Marx was busy writing other works and, to some extent, because the contract with the publisher was cancelled in September 1846, the latter being afraid to have transactions with such a revolutionary-minded author. However, in the early 1850s Marx returned to the idea of writing a book on economics. Thus, the manuscripts of 1844 are connected with the conception of a plan which led many years later to the writing of *Capital*.

The *Economic and Philosophic Manuscripts* is an unfinished work and in part a rough draft. A considerable part of the text has not been preserved. What remains comprises three manuscripts, each of which has its own pagination (in Roman figures). The first manuscript contains 27 pages, of which pages I-XII and XVII-XXVII are divided by two vertical lines into three columns supplied with headings written in beforehand: "Wages of Labour," "Profit of Capital" (this section has also subheadings supplied by the author) and "Rent of Land." It is difficult to tell the order in which Marx filled these columns. All the three columns on p. VII contain the text relating to the section "Wages of Labour." Pages XIII to XVI are divided into two columns and contain texts of the sections "Wages of Labour" (pp. XIII-XV), "Profit of Capital" (pp. XIII-XVI) and "Rent of Land" (p. XVI). On pages XVII to XXI, only the column headed "Rent of Land" is filled in. From page XXII to page XXVII, on which the first manuscript breaks off, Marx wrote across the three columns disregarding the headings. The text of these pages is published as a separate section entitled by the editors according to its content "Estranged Labour."

Of the second manuscript only the last four pages have survived (pp. XL-XLIII).

The third manuscript contains 41 pages (not counting blank ones) divided into two columns and numbered by Marx himself from I to XLIII (in doing so he omitted two numbers, XXII and XXV). Like the extant part of the second manuscript, the third manuscript has no author's headings; the text has been arranged and supplied with the headings by the editors.

Sometimes Marx departed from the subject-matter and interrupted his elucidation of one question to analyse another. Pages XXXIX-XL contain the Preface to the whole work which is given before the text of the first manuscript. The text of the section dealing with the critical analysis of Hegel's dialectic, to which Marx referred in the Preface as the concluding chapter and which was scattered on various pages, is arranged in one section and put at the end in accordance with Marx's indications.

In order to give the reader a better visual idea of the structure of the work, the text reproduces in vertical lines the Roman numbers of the sheets of the manuscripts, and the Arabic numbers of the columns in the first manuscript. The notes indicate where the text has been rearranged. Passages crossed out by Marx with a vertical line are enclosed in pointed brackets; separate words or phrases crossed out by the author are given in footnotes only when they supplement the text. The general title and the headings of the various parts of the manuscripts enclosed in square brackets are supplied by the editors on the basis of the author's formulations. In some places the text has been broken up into paragraphs by the editors. Quotations from the French sources cited by Marx in French or in his own translation into German, are given in English in both cases and the French texts as quoted by Marx are given in the footnotes. Here and elsewhere Marx's rendering of the quotations or free translation is given in small type but without quotation marks. Emphasis in quotations, belonging, as a rule, to Marx, as well as that of the quoted authors, is indicated everywhere by italics.

The *Economic and Philosophic Manuscripts of 1844* was first published by the Institute of Marxism-Leninism in Moscow in the language of the original: Marx/Engels, *Gesamtausgabe, Abt.* 1, Bd. 3, 1932.

In English this work was first published in 1959 by the Foreign Languages Publishing House (now Progress Publishers), Moscow, translated by Martin Milligan.

attempt a critique of the speculative elaboration of that material. For this reason it will be found that the interconnection between political economy and the state, law, ethics, civil life, etc., is touched upon in the present work only to the extent to which political economy itself expressly touches upon these subjects.

It is hardly necessary to assure the reader conversant with political economy that my results have been attained by means of a wholly empirical analysis based on a conscientious critical study of political economy.

(Whereas the uninformed reviewer who tries to hide his complete ignorance and intellectual poverty by hurling the "*utopian phrase*" at the positive critic's head, or again such phrases as "quite pure, quite resolute, quite critical criticism," the "not merely legal but social—utterly social—society," the "compact, massy mass," the "outspoken spokesmen of the massy mass,"[2] this reviewer has yet to furnish the first proof that besides his theological family affairs he has anything to contribute to a discussion of *worldly* matters.)

It goes without saying that besides the French and English socialists I have also used German socialist works. The only original German works of substance in this science, however—other than Weitling's writings—are the essays by *Hess* published in *Einundzwanzig Bogen*[3] and *Umrisse zu einer Kritik der Nationalökonomie by* Engels in the *Deutsch-Französische Jahrbücher,* where also the basic elements of this work have been indicated by me in a very general way.

(Besides being indebted to these authors who have given critical attention to political economy, positive criticism as a whole—and therefore also German positive criticism of political economy—owes its true foundation to the discoveries of *Feuerbach*, against whose *Philosophie der Zukunft* and *Thesen zur Reform der Philosophie* in the *Anekdota,* despite the tacit use that is made of them, the petty envy of some and the veritable wrath of others seem to have instigated a regular conspiracy of *silence.*

It is only with *Feuerbach* that *positive,* humanistic and naturalistic criticism begins. The less noise they make, the more certain, profound, extensive, and enduring is the effect of *Feuerbach's* writings, the only writings since Hegel's *Phänomenologie* and *Logik* to contain a real theoretical revolution.

In contrast to the *critical theologians* of our day, I have deemed the concluding chapter of this work—a critical discussion of *Hegelian dialectic* and philosophy as a whole to be absolutely necessary, a task not yet performed. This *lack of thoroughness* is not accidental, since even the *critical* theologian remains a *theologian.* Hence, either he has to start from certain presuppositions of philosophy accepted as authoritative; or, if in the process of criticism and as a result of other people's discoveries doubts about these philosophical presuppositions have arisen in him, he abandons them in a cowardly and unwarrantable fashion, *abstracts* from them, thus showing his servile dependence on

---

[2] This refers to Bruno Bauer's reviews of books, articles and pamphlets on the Jewish question, including Marx's article on the subject in the *Deutsch-Französche Jahrbücher,* which were published in the monthly *Allgemeine Literatur-Zeitung* (issue No. 1, December 1843, and issue No. IV, March 1844) under the title "*Von den neuesten Schriften über die Judenfrage."* Most of the expressions quoted are taken from these reviews. The expressions "utopian phrase" and "compact mass" can he found in Bruno Bauer's unsigned article, "*Was ist jetzt der Gegenstand der Kritik?*," published in the *Allgemeine Literatur-Zeitung,* issue No. VIII, July 1844. A detailed critical appraisal of this monthly was later on given by Marx and Engels in the book *Die heilige Familie, oder Kritik der kritischen Kritik* (see this edition, Vol. 4, *The Holy Family, or Critique of Critical Criticism).*

[3] Marx apparently refers to Weitling's works: *Die Menschheit, wie sie ist und wie sie sein sollte,* 1838, and *Garantien der Harmonic und Freiheit,* Vivis, 1842.

Moses Hess published three articles in the collection *Ein-und-zwanzig Bogen aus der Schweiz* (Twenty-One Sheets from Switzerland), *Erster Teil (Zürich und Winterthur,* 1843), issued by Georg Herwegh. These articles, entitled "*Sozialismus und Kommunismus,*" "*Philosophie der Tat*" and "*Die Eine und die ganze Freiheit,*" were published anonymously. The first two of them had a note—"Written by the author of 'Europäische Triarchie.'"

these presuppositions and his resentment at this servility merely in a negative, unconscious and sophistical manner.

(He does this either by constantly repeating assurances concerning the *purity* of his own criticism, or by trying to make it seem as though all that was left for criticism to deal with now was some other limited form of criticism outside itself—say eighteenth-century criticism—and also the limitations of the *masses,* in order to divert the observer's attention as well as his own from the *necessary* task of settling accounts between *criticism* and its point of origin—Hegelian *dialectic* and German philosophy as a whole—that is, from this necessary raising of modern criticism above its own limitation and crudity. Eventually, however, whenever discoveries (such as *Feuerbach's*) are made regarding the nature of his own philosophic presuppositions, the critical theologian partly makes it appear as if *he* were the one who had accomplished this, producing that appearance by taking the results of these discoveries and, without being able to develop them, hurling them in the form of *catch-phrases* at writers still caught in the confines of philosophy. He partly even manages to acquire a sense of his own superiority to such discoveries by asserting in a mysterious way and in a veiled, malicious and skeptical fashion elements of the Hegelian *dialectic* which he still finds lacking in the criticism of that dialectic (which have not yet been critically served up to him for his use) against such criticism—not having tried to bring such elements into their proper relation or having been capable of doing so, asserting, say, the category of mediating proof against the category of positive, self-originating truth, (...) in a way *peculiar* to Hegelian dialectic. For to the theological critic it seems quite natural that everything has to be *done* by philosophy, so that he can *chatter away* about purity, resoluteness, and quite critical criticism; and he fancies himself the true *conqueror of philosophy* whenever he happens to *feel* some element[4] in Hegel to be lacking in Feuerbach—for however much he practises the spiritual idolatry of "*self-consciousness*" and "mind" the theological critic does not get beyond feeling to consciousness.)

On close inspection *theological* criticism—genuinely progressive though it was at the inception of the movement—is seen in the final analysis to be nothing but the culmination and consequence of the old *philosophical,* and especially the *Hegelian, transcendentalism,* twisted into a *theological caricature.* This interesting example of historical justice, which now assigns to theology, ever philosophy's spot of infection, the further role of portraying in itself the negative dissolution of philosophy, i.e., the process of its decay—this historical nemesis I shall demonstrate on another occasion.[5]

(How far, on the other hand, *Feuerbach's* discoveries about the nature of philosophy still, for their *proof* at least, called for a critical discussion of philosophical dialectic will be seen from my exposition itself.)

---

[4] The term "element" in the Hegelian philosophy means a vital element of thought. It is used to stress that thought is a process, and that therefore elements in a system of thought are also phases in a movement. The term "feeling" (*Empfindung*) denotes relatively low forms of mental life in which no distinction is made between the subjective and objective.
[5] Shortly after writing this Preface Marx fulfilled his intention in *The Holy Family, or Critique of Critical Criticism,* written in collaboration with Engels (see Karl Marx and Frederick Engels, *Collected Works,* Vol. 4).

WAGES OF LABOUR

Wages are determined through the antagonistic struggle between capitalist and worker. Victory goes necessarily to the capitalist. The capitalist can live longer without the worker than can the worker without the capitalist. Combination among the capitalists is customary and effective; workers' combination is prohibited and painful in its consequences for them. Besides, the landowner and the capitalist can make use of industrial advantages to augment their revenues; the worker has neither rent nor interest on capital to supplement his industrial income. Hence the intensity of the competition among the workers. Thus only for the workers is the separation of capital, landed property, and labour an inevitable, essential and detrimental separation. Capital and landed property need not remain fixed in this abstraction, as must the labour of the workers.

The separation of capital, rent, and labour is thus fatal for the worker.

The lowest and the only necessary wage rate is that providing for the subsistence of the worker for the duration of his work and as much more as is necessary for him to support a family and for the race of labourers not to die out. The ordinary wage, according to Smith, is the lowest compatible with common humanity,[6] that is, with cattle-like existence.

The demand for men necessarily governs the production of men, as of every other commodity. Should supply greatly exceed demand, a section of the workers sinks into beggary or starvation. The worker's existence is thus brought under the same condition as the existence of every other commodity. The worker has become a commodity, and it is a bit of luck for him if he can find a buyer. And the demand on which the life of the worker depends, depends on the whim of the rich and the capitalists. Should supply exceed demand, then one of the constituent parts of the price—profit, rent or wages—is paid below its *rate*, [a part of these] factors is therefore withdrawn from this application, and thus the market price gravitates [towards the] natural price as the centre-point. But (1) where there is considerable division of labour it is most difficult for the worker to direct his labour into other channels; (2) because of his subordinate relation to the capitalist, he is the first to suffer.

Thus in the gravitation of market price to natural price it is the worker who loses most of all and necessarily. And it is just the capacity of the capitalist to direct his capital into another channel which either renders the worker, who is restricted to some particular branch of labour, destitute, or forces him to submit to every demand of this capitalist.

The accidental and sudden fluctuations in market price hit rent less than they do that part of the price which is resolved into profit and wages; but they hit profit less than they do wages. In most cases, for every wage that rises, one remains *stationary* and one *falls*.

The worker need not necessarily gain when the capitalist does, but he necessarily loses when the latter loses. Thus, the worker does not gain if the capitalist keeps the market price above the natural price by virtue of some manufacturing or trading secret, or by virtue of monopoly or the favorable situation of his land.

Furthermore, *the prices of labour are much more constant than the prices of*

---

[6] The expression "common humanity" (in the manuscript in French, "simple humanity") was borrowed by Marx from the first volume (Chapter VIII) of Adam Smith's *Wealth of Nations*, which he used in Garnier's French translation *(Recherches sur la nature et les causes de la richesse des nations,* Paris, 1802, t. I, p. 138). All the subsequent references were given by Marx to this publication, the synopsis of which is contained in his Paris Notebooks with excerpts on political economy. This edition is reproduced on the MIA and Marx's citations are linked to the text.

provisions. Often they stand in inverse proportion. In a dear year wages fall on account of the decrease in demand, but rise on account of the increase in the prices of provisions—and thus balance. In any case, a number of workers are left without bread. In cheap years wages rise on account of the rise in demand, but decrease on account of the fall in the prices of provisions—and thus balance.

Another respect in which the worker is at a disadvantage:

The labour prices of the various kinds of workers show much wider differences than the profits in the various branches in which capital is applied. In labour all the natural, spiritual, and social variety of individual activity is manifested and is variously rewarded, whilst dead capital always keeps the same pace and is indifferent to real individual activity.

In general we should observe that in those cases where worker and capitalist equally suffer, the worker suffers in his very existence, the capitalist in the profit on his dead mammon.

The worker has to struggle not only for his physical means of subsistence; he has to struggle to get work, i.e., the possibility, the means, to perform his activity.

Let us take the three chief conditions in which society can find itself and consider the situation of the worker in them:

(1) If the wealth of society declines the worker suffers most of all, and for the following reason: although the working class cannot gain so much as can the class of property owners in a prosperous state of society, *no one suffers so cruelly from its decline as the working class.*

(2) Let us now take a society in which wealth is increasing. This condition is the only one favorable to the worker. Here competition between the capitalists sets in. The demand for workers exceeds their supply. But:

In the first place, the raising of wages gives rise to overwork among the workers. The more they wish to earn, the more must they sacrifice their time and carry out slave-labour, completely losing all their freedom, in the service of greed. Thereby they shorten their lives. This shortening of their life-span is a favourable circumstance for the working class as a whole, for as a result of it an ever-fresh supply of labour becomes necessary. This class has always to sacrifice a part of itself in order not to be wholly destroyed.

Furthermore: When does a society find itself in a condition of advancing wealth? When the capitals and the revenues of a country are growing. But this is only possible:

(a) As the result of the accumulation of much labour, capital being accumulated labour; as the result, therefore, of the fact that more and more of his products are being taken away from the worker, that to an increasing extent his own labour confronts him as another man's property and that the means of his existence and his activity are increasingly concentrated in the hands of the capitalist.

(b) The accumulation of capital increases the division of labour, and the division of labour increases the number of workers. Conversely, the number of workers increases the division of labour, just as the division of labour increases the accumulation of capital. With this division of labour on the one hand and the accumulation of capital on the other, the worker becomes ever more exclusively dependent on labour, and on a particular, very one-sided, machine-like labour at that. Just as he is thus depressed spiritually and physically to the condition of a machine and from being a man becomes an abstract activity and a belly, so he also becomes ever more dependent on every fluctuation in market price, on the application of capital, and on the whim of the rich. Equally, the increase in the class of people wholly dependent on work intensifies competition among the workers, thus lowering their price. In the factory system this situation of the worker reaches its climax.

(c) In an increasingly prosperous society only the richest of the rich can continue to live on money interest. Everyone else has to carry on a business with his capital, or venture it in trade. As a result, the competition between the capitalists becomes more intense. The concentration of capital increases, the big capitalists ruin the small, and a section of the erstwhile capitalists sinks into the working class, which as a result of this supply again suffers to some extent a depression of wages and passes into a still greater dependence on the few big capitalists. The number of capitalists having been diminished, their competition with respect to the workers scarcely exists any longer; and the number of workers having been increased, their competition among themselves has become all the more intense, unnatural, and violent. Consequently, a section of the working class falls into beggary or starvation just as necessarily as a section of the middle capitalists falls into the working class.

Hence even in the condition of society most favorable to the worker, the inevitable result for the worker is overwork and premature death, decline to a mere machine, a bond servant of capital, which piles up dangerously over and against him, more competition, and starvation or beggary for a section of the workers.

The raising of wages excites in the worker the capitalist's mania to get rich, which he, however, can only satisfy by the sacrifice of his mind and body. The raising of wages presupposes and entails the accumulation of capital, and thus sets the product of labour against the worker as something ever more alien to him. Similarly, the division of labour renders him ever more one-sided and dependent, bringing with it the competition not only of men but also of machines. Since the worker has sunk to the level of a machine, he can be confronted by the machine as a competitor. Finally, as the amassing of capital increases the amount of industry and therefore the number of workers, it causes the same amount of industry to manufacture *a larger amount of products*, which leads to over-production and thus either ends by throwing a large section of workers out of work or by reducing their wages to the most miserable minimum.

Such are the consequences of a state of society most favourable to the worker— namely, of a state of *growing, advancing* wealth.

Eventually, however, this state of growth must sooner or later reach its peak. What is the worker's position now?

(3) "In a country which had acquired that full complement of riches both the wages of labour and the profits of stock would probably be very low. The competition for employment would necessarily be so great as to reduce the wages of labour to what was barely sufficient to keep up the number of labourers, and, the country being already fully peopled, that number could never be augmented."[7]

The surplus would have to die.

Thus in a declining state of society—increasing misery of the worker; in an advancing state—misery with complications; and in a fully developed state of society— static misery.

Since, however, according to Smith, a society is not happy, of which the greater part suffers—yet even the wealthiest state of society leads to this suffering of the majority—

---

[7] Adam Smith, *Wealth of Nations*, Vol. I, p. 84.

and since the *economic system*[8] (and in general a society based on private interest) leads to this wealthiest condition, it follows that the goal of the economic system is the *unhappiness* of society.

Concerning the relationship between worker and capitalist we should add that the capitalist is more than compensated for rising wages by the reduction in the amount of labour time, and that rising wages and rising interest on capital operate on the price of commodities like simple and compound interest respectively.

Let us put ourselves now wholly at the standpoint of the political economist, and follow him in comparing the theoretical and practical claims of the workers.

He tells us that originally and in theory the *whole product* of labour belongs to the worker. But at the same time he tells us that in actual fact what the worker gets is the smallest and utterly indispensable part of the product—as much, only, as is necessary for his existence, not as a human being, but as a worker, and for the propagation, not of humanity, but of the slave class of workers.

The political economist tells us that everything is bought with labour and that capital is nothing but accumulated labour; but at the same time he tells us that the worker, far from being able to buy everything, must sell himself and his humanity.

Whilst the rent of the idle landowner usually amounts to a third of the product of the soil, and the profit of the busy capitalist to as much as twice the interest on money, the "something more" which the worker himself earns at the best of times amounts to so little that of four children of his, two must starve and die.

Whilst according to the political economists it is solely through labour that man enhances the value of the products of nature, whilst labour is man's active possession, according to this same political economy the landowner and the capitalist, who *qua* landowner and capitalist are merely privileged and idle gods, are everywhere superior to the worker and lay down the law to him.

Whilst according to the political economists labour is the sole unchanging price of things, there is nothing more fortuitous than the price of labour, nothing exposed to greater fluctuations.

Whilst the division of labour raises the productive power of labour and increases the wealth and refinement of society, it impoverishes the worker and reduces him to a machine. Whilst labour brings about the accumulation of capital and with this the increasing prosperity of society, it renders the worker ever more dependent on the capitalist, leads him into competition of a new intensity, and drives him into the headlong rush of overproduction, with its subsequent corresponding slump.

Whilst the interest of the worker, according to the political economists, never stands opposed to the interest of society, society always and necessarily stands opposed to the interest of the worker.

According to the political economists, the interest of the worker is never opposed to that of society: (1) because the rising wages are more than compensated by the reduction in the amount of labour time, together with the other consequences set forth above; and (2) because in relation to society the whole gross product is the net product, and only in relation to the private individual has the net product any significance.

But that labour itself, not merely in present conditions but insofar as its purpose in general is the mere increase of wealth—that labour itself, I say, is harmful and pernicious—follows from the political economist's line of argument, without his being

---

[8] Marx uses the German term "Nationalökonomie" to denote both the economic system in the sense of science or theory, and the economic system itself.

aware of it.

In theory, rent of land and profit on capital are *deductions* suffered by wages. In actual fact, however, wages are a deduction which land and capital allow to go to the worker, a concession from the product of labour to the workers, to labour.

When society is in a state of decline, the worker suffers most severely. The specific severity of his burden he owes to his position as a worker, but the burden as such to the position of society.

But when society is in a state of progress, the ruin and impoverishment of the worker is the product of his labour and of the wealth produced by him. The misery results, therefore, from the *essence* of present-day labour itself.

Society in a state of maximum wealth—an ideal, but one which is approximately attained, and which at least is the aim of political economy as of civil society—means for the workers *static misery*.

It goes without saying that the *proletarian*, i.e., the man who, being without capital and rent, lives purely by labour, and by a one-sided, abstract labour, is considered by political economy only as a *worker*. Political economy can therefore advance the proposition that the proletarian, the same as any horse, must get as much as will enable him to work. It does not consider him when he is not working, as a human being; but leaves such consideration to criminal law, to doctors, to religion, to the statistical tables, to politics and to the poor-house overseer.

Let us now rise above the level of political economy and try to answer two questions on the basis of the above exposition, which has been presented almost in the words of the political economists:

(1) What in the evolution of mankind is the meaning of this reduction of the greater part of mankind to abstract labour?

(2) What are the mistakes committed by the piecemeal reformers, who either want to raise wages and in this way to improve the situation of the working class, or regard equality of wages (as Proudhon does) as the goal of social revolution?

In political economy labour occurs only in the form of *activity as a source of livelihood*.

"It can be asserted that those occupations which presuppose specific talents or longer training have become on the whole more lucrative; whilst the proportionate reward for mechanically monotonous activity in which one person can be trained as easily and quickly as another has fallen with growing competition, and was inevitably bound to fall. And it is just *this* sort of work which in the present state of the organization of labour is still by far the commonest. If therefore a worker in the first category now earns seven times as much as he did, say, fifty years ago, whilst the earnings of another in the second category have remained unchanged, then of course both are earning *on the average* four times as much. But if the first category comprises only a thousand workers in a particular country, and the second a million, then 999,000 are no better off than fifty years ago— and they are *worse off* if at the same time the prices of the necessaries of life have risen. With such superficial *calculation of averages* people try to deceive themselves about the most numerous class of the population. Moreover, the size of the *wage* is only one factor in the estimation of the *worker's* income, because it is essential for the measurement of the latter to take into account the certainty of its *duration*—which is obviously out of the question in the anarchy of so-called free competition, with its ever-recurring fluctuations and periods of stagnation. Finally, the *hours of work* customary formerly and now have to be considered. And for the English cotton-workers these have been increased, as a result of the entrepreneurs' mania for profit, to between twelve and sixteen hours a day during the past twenty-five years or so—that is to say, precisely during the period of the introduction of labour-saving machines; and this increase in one country and in one branch of industry inevitably asserted itself elsewhere to a greater or lesser degree, for the right of the unlimited exploitation of the poor by the rich is still universally recognized." (Wilhelm Schulz, *Die Bewegung der Production.*)

"But even if it were as true as it is false that the average income of *every* class of society has increased, the income-differences and *relative* income-distances may nevertheless have become greater and the contrasts between wealth and poverty accordingly stand out more sharply. For just because total production rises—and in the same measure as it rises—needs, desires and claims also multiply and thus *relative* poverty can increase whilst *absolute* poverty diminishes. The Samoyed living on fish oil and rancid fish is not poor because in his secluded society all have the same needs. But in a state *that is forging ahead*, which in the course of a decade, say, increased by a third its total production in proportion to the population, the worker who is getting as much at the end of ten years as at the beginning has not remained as well off, but has become poorer by a third." (Ibid., pp. 65-66)

But political economy knows the worker only as a working animal—as a beast reduced to the strictest bodily needs.

"To develop in greater spiritual freedom, a people must break their bondage to their bodily needs—they must cease to be the slaves of the body. They must, above all, have *time* at their disposal for spiritual creative activity and spiritual enjoyment. The developments in the labour organism gain this time. Indeed, with new motive forces and improved machinery, a single worker in the cotton mills now often performs the work formerly requiring a hundred, or even 250 to 350 workers. Similar results can be observed in all branches of production, because external natural forces are being compelled to participate to an ever-greater degree in human labour. If the satisfaction of a given amount of material needs formerly required a certain expenditure of time and human effort which has later been reduced by half, then without any loss of material comfort the scope for spiritual activity and enjoyment has been simultaneously extended by as much.... But again the way in which the booty, that we win from old Cronus [Greek God associated with time.] himself in his most private domain, is shared out is still decided by the dice-throw of blind, unjust Chance. In France it has been calculated that at the present stage in the development of production an average working period of five hours a day by every person capable of work could suffice for the satisfaction of all the material interests of society.... Notwithstanding the time saved by the perfecting of machinery. the duration of the slave-labour performed by a large population in the factories has only increased." (Schulz, Ibid., pp. 67, 68.)

"The transition from compound manual labour rests on a break-down of the latter into its simple operations. At first, however, only *some* of the uniformly-recurring operations will devolve on machines, while some will devolve on men. From the nature of things, and from confirmatory experience, it is clear that unendingly monotonous activity of this kind is as harmful to the mind as to the body; thus this *combination* of machinery with mere division of labour among a greater number of hands must inevitably show all the disadvantages of the latter. These disadvantages appear, among other things, in the greater mortality of factory workers.... Consideration has not been given ... to this big distinction as to how far men work *through* machines or how far *as* machines." (Ibid., p. 69.)

"In the future life of the peoples, however, the inanimate forces of nature working in machines will be our slaves and serfs." (Ibid., p. 74.)

"The English spinning mills employ 196,818 women and only 158,818 men. For every 100 male workers in the cotton mills of Lancashire there are 103 female workers, and in Scotland as many as 209. In the English flax mills of Leeds, for every 100 male workers there were found to be 147 female workers. In Dundee and on the east coast of Scotland as many as 280. In the English silk mills ... many female workers; male workers predominate in the woollen mills where the work requires greater physical strength. In 1833, no fewer than 38,927 women were employed alongside 18,593 men in the North American cotton mills. As a result of the changes in the labour organism, a wider sphere of gainful employment has thus fallen to the share of the female sex.... Women now occupying an economically more independent position ... the two sexes are drawn closer together in their social conditions." (Ibid., pp. 71-72.)

"Working in the English steam- and water-driven spinning mills in 1835 were: 20,558 children between the ages of eight and twelve; 35,867 between the ages of twelve and thirteen; and, lastly, 108,208 children between the ages of thirteen and eighteen.... Admittedly, further advances in mechanisation, by more and more removing all monotonous work from human hands, are operating in the direction of a gradual elimination of this evil. But standing in the way of these more rapid advances is the very circumstance that the capitalists can, in the easiest and cheapest fashion, appropriate the energies of the lower classes down to the children, to be used *instead* of mechanical devices." (Ibid., pp. 70-71.)

"Lord Brougham's call to the workers—'Become capitalists'. ... This is the evil that millions are able to earn a bare subsistence for themselves only by strenuous labour which shatters the body and cripples them morally and intellectually; that they are even obliged to consider the misfortune of finding *such* work a piece of good fortune." (Ibid., p. 60.)

"In order to live, then, the non-owners are obliged to place themselves, directly or indirectly, *at the service* of the owners—to put themselves, that is to say, into a position of dependence upon them." (Pecqueur, *Théorie nouvelle d'économie soc., etc.*.)

Servants—pay: workers—wages; employees—salary or *emoluments.* (*loc. cit.*, pp. 409, 410.)

"To hire out one's labour," "to lend one's labour at interest," "to work in another's place."

"To hire out the materials of labour", "to lend the materials of labour at interest", "to make others work in one's place". (Ibid., p. 411.)

"Such an economic order condemns men to occupations so mean, to a degradation so devastating and bitter, that by comparison savagery seems like a kingly condition.... (Ibid., pp. 417, 418.) "Prostitution of the non-owning class in all its forms." (Ibid., p. 421 f.) "Ragmen."

Charles Loudon in the book *Solution du probleme de la population, etc.*, Paris,

1842,[9] declares the number of prostitutes in England to be between sixty and seventy thousand. The number of women of doubtful virtue is said to be equally large (p. 228).

"The average life of these unfortunate creatures on the streets, after they have embarked on their career of vice, is about six or seven years. To maintain the number of sixty to seventy thousand prostitutes, there must be in the three kingdoms at least eight to nine thousand women who commit themselves to this abject profession each year, or about twenty-four new victims each day—an average of *one* per hour; and it follows that if the same proportion holds good over the whole surface of the globe, there must constantly be in existence one and a half million unfortunate women of this kind." (Ibid., p. 229.)

"The numbers of the poverty-stricken grow with their poverty, and at the extreme limit of destitution human beings are crowded together in the greatest numbers contending with each other for the right to suffer.... In 1821 the population of Ireland was 6,801,827. In 1831 it had risen to 7,764,010—an increase of 14 per cent in ten years. In Leinster, the wealthiest province, the population increased by only 8 per cent; whilst in Connaught, the most poverty-stricken province, the increase reached 21 per cent. (Extract from the *Enquiries Published in England on Ireland*, Vienna, 1840.)" (Buret, *De la misère*, etc., t. 1, pp. 36, 37.)

Political economy considers labour in the abstract as a thing; labour is a commodity. If the price is high, then the commodity is in great demand; if the price is low, then the commodity is in great supply: the price of labour as a commodity must fall lower and lower. This is made inevitable partly by the competition between capitalist and worker, partly by the competition amongst the workers. "The working population, the seller of labour, is necessarily reduced to accepting the most meagre part of the product.... Is the theory of labour as a commodity anything other than a theory of disguised bondage?" (*Ibid.* p. 43.) "Why then has nothing but an exchange-value been seen in labour?" (Ibid., p. 44.) The large workshops prefer to buy the labour of women and children, because this costs less than that of men. (Ibid.) "The worker is not at all in the position of a free seller vis-à-vis the one who employs him.... The capitalist is always free to employ labour, and the worker is always forced to sell it. The value of labour is completely destroyed if it is not sold every instant. Labour can neither be accumulated nor even be saved, unlike true [commodities]. "Labour is life, and if life is not each day exchanged for food, it suffers and soon perishes. To claim that human life is a commodity, one must, therefore, admit slavery." (Ibid., p. 49, 50.) If then labour is a commodity it is a commodity with the most unfortunate attributes. But even by the principles of political economy it is no commodity, for it is not the "*free result of a free transaction*." The present economic regime "simultaneously lowers the price and the remuneration of labour; it perfects the worker and degrades the man." (Ibid., pp. 52-53.) "Industry has become a war, and commerce a gamble." (Ibid., p. 62.)

"The cotton-working machines" (in England) alone represent 84,000,000 manual workers. (Ibid., p. 193.)

Up to the present, industry has been in a state of war, a war of conquest: "It has squandered the lives of the men who made up its army with the same indifference as the great conquerors. Its aim was the possession of wealth, not the happiness of men." (Buret,

---

[9] Loudon's work was a translation into French of an English manuscript apparently never published in the original. The author did publish in English a short pamphlet—*The Equilibrium of Population and Sustenance Demonstrated*, Leamington, 1836.

Ibid.) "These interests" (that is, economic interests), "freely left to themselves ... must necessarily come into conflict; they have no other arbiter but war, and the decisions of war assign defeat and death to some, in order to give victory to the others.... It is in the conflict of opposed forces that science seeks order and equilibrium: *perpetual war*, according to it, is the sole means of obtaining peace; that war is called competition." (Ibid., p. 23.)

"The industrial war, to be conducted with success, demands large armies which it can amass on one spot and profusely decimate. And it is neither from devotion nor from duty that the soldiers of this army bear the exertions imposed on them, but only to escape the hard necessity of hunger. They feel neither attachment nor gratitude towards their bosses, nor are these bound to their subordinates by any feeling of benevolence. They do not know them as men, but only as instruments of production which have to yield as much as possible with as little cost as possible. These populations of workers, ever more crowded together, have not even the assurance of always being employed. Industry, which has called them together, only lets them live while it needs them, and as soon as it can get rid of them it abandons them without the slightest scruple; and the workers are compelled to offer their persons and their powers for whatever price they can get. The longer, more painful and more disgusting the work they are given, the less they are paid. There are those who, with sixteen hours' work a day and unremitting exertion, scarcely buy the right not to die." (Ibid., pp. 68-69.)

"We are convinced ... as are the commissioners charged with the inquiry into the condition of the hand-loom weavers, that the large industrial towns would in a short time lose their population of workers if they were not all the time receiving from the neighbouring rural areas constant recruitments of healthy men, a constant flow of fresh blood." (Ibid., p. 362.)

PROFIT OF CAPITAL

1. Capital

What is the basis of *capital*, that is, of private property in the products of other men's labour?

"Even if capital itself does not merely amount to theft or fraud, it still requires the cooperation of legislation to sanctify inheritance." (Say, *Traité d'économie politique.*)[10]

How does one become a proprietor of productive stock? How does one become owner of the products created by means of this stock?
By virtue of *positive law*. (Say, t. II, p. 4.)
What does one acquire with capital, with the inheritance of a large fortune, for instance?

"The person who [either acquires, or] succeeds to a great fortune, does not necessarily [acquire or] succeed to any political power.... The power which that possession immediately and directly conveys to him, is the *power of purchasing*; a certain command over all the labour, or over all the produce of labour, which is then in the

---

[10] Unlike the quotations from a number of other French writers such as Constantin Pecqueur and Eugéne Buret, which Marx gives in French in this work, the excerpts from J. B. Say's book are given in his German translation.

market." (*Wealth of Nations* by Adam Smith, Vol. I, pp. 26-27.)[11]

Capital is thus the *governing power* over labour and its products. The capitalist possesses this power, not on account of his personal or human qualities, but inasmuch as he is an *owner* of capital. His power is the *purchasing* power of his capital, which nothing can withstand.

Later we shall see first how the capitalist, by means of capital, exercises his governing power over labour, then, however, we shall see the governing power of capital over the capitalist himself.

What is capital?

"A certain quantity of *labour stocked* and stored up to be employed." (Adam Smith, Ibid., Vol. I, p. 295.)

Capital is *stored-up labour*.

(2) *Fonds*, or stock, is any accumulation of products of the soil or of manufacture. Stock is called *capital* only when it yields to its owner a revenue or profit. (Adam Smith, Ibid., p. 243)

2. The Profit of Capital

The *profit* or *gain of capital* is altogether different from the *wages of labour*. This difference is manifested in two ways: in the first place, the profits of capital are regulated altogether by the value of the capital employed, although the labour of inspection and direction associated with different capitals may be the same. Moreover in large works the whole of this labour is committed to some principal clerk, whose salary bears no regular proportion to the capital of which he oversees the management. And although the labour of the proprietor is here reduced almost to nothing, he still demands profits in proportion to his capital. (Adam Smith, Ibid., Vol. I, p. 43)[12]

Why does the capitalist demand this proportion between profit and capital?

He would have no *interest* in employing the workers, unless he expected from the sale of their work something more than is necessary to replace the stock advanced by him as wages and he would have no *interest* to employ a great stock rather than a small one, unless his profits were to bear some proportion to the extent of his stock. (Adam Smith, Ibid., Vol. I, p. 42)

The capitalist thus makes a profit, first, on the wages, and secondly on the raw materials advanced by him.

What proportion, then, does profit bear to capital?

If it is already difficult to determine the usual average level of wages at a particular place and at a particular time, it is even more difficult to determine the profit on capitals.

---

[11] From this page of the manuscript quotations from Adam Smith's book (in the French translation), which Marx cited so far sometimes in French and sometimes in German, are, as a rule, given in German. In this book the corresponding pages of the English edition are substituted for the French by the editors and Marx's references are given in square brackets (see Note 6).

[12] The text published in small type here and below is not an exact quotation from Smith but a summary of the corresponding passages from his work. Such passages are subsequently given in small type but without quotation marks.

A change in the price of the commodities in which the capitalist deals, the good or bad fortune of his rivals and customers, a thousand other accidents to which commodities are exposed both in transit and in the warehouses—all produce a daily, almost hourly variation in profit. (Adam Smith, Ibid., Vol. I, pp. 78-79.)

But though it is impossible to determine with precision what are the profits on capitals, some notion may be formed of them from the *interest of money*. Wherever a great deal can be made by the use of money, a great deal will be given for the use of it; wherever little can be made by it, little will be given. (Adam Smith, Ibid., Vol. I, p. 79.)

The proportion which the usual market rate of interest ought to bear to the rate of clear profit, necessarily varies as profit rises or falls. Double interest is in Great Britain reckoned what the merchants call a good, moderate, reasonable profit, terms which mean no more than a *common and usual profit*. (Adam Smith, Ibid., Vol. I, p. 87.)

What is the *lowest* rate of profit? And what the *highest?*

The *lowest* rate of ordinary profit on capital must always be *something more* than what is sufficient to compensate the occasional losses to which every employment of stock is exposed. It is this surplus only which is neat or clear profit. The same holds for the lowest rate of interest. (Adam Smith, Ibid., Vol. I, p. 86)

The *highest* rate to which ordinary profits can rise is that which in the price of the greater part of commodities eats *up the whole of the* rent *of the* land, and reduces the wages of labour contained in the commodity supplied to the *lowest rate,* the bare subsistence of the labourer during his work. The worker must always be fed in some way or other while he is required to work; rent can disappear entirely. For example: the servants of the East India Company in Bengal. (Adam Smith, Ibid., Vol. I, pp. 86-87)

Besides all the advantages of limited competition which the capitalist may *exploit* in this case, he can keep the market price above the natural price by quite decorous means.

For one thing, by keeping *secrets in trade* if the market is at a great distance from those who supply it, that is, by concealing a price change, its rise above the natural level. This concealment has the effect that other capitalists do not follow him in investing their capital in this branch of industry or trade.

Then again by keeping *secrets in manufacture*, which enable the capitalist to reduce the costs of production and supply his commodity at the same or even at lower prices than his competitors while obtaining a higher profit. (Deceiving by keeping secrets is not immoral? Dealings on the Stock Exchange.) *Furthermore*, where production is restricted to a particular locality (as in the case of a rare wine), and where the *effective demand* can never be satisfied. *Finally*, through *monopolies* exercised by individuals or companies. Monopoly price is the highest possible. (Adam Smith, Ibid., Vol. I, pp. 53-54)

Other fortuitous causes which can raise the profit on capital:

The acquisition of new territories, or of new branches of trade, often increases the profit on capital even in a wealthy country, because they withdraw some capital from the old branches of trade, reduce competition, and cause the market to be supplied with fewer commodities, the prices of which then rise: those who deal in these commodities can then afford to borrow at a higher rate of interest. (Adam Smith, Ibid., Vol. I, p. 83)

The more a commodity comes to be manufactured—the more it becomes an object of manufacture—the greater becomes that part of the price which resolves itself into wages and profit in proportion to that which resolves itself into rent. In the progress of the manufacture of a commodity, not only the number of profits increases, but every subsequent profit is greater than the foregoing; because the capital from which it is derived must always be greater. The capital which employs the weavers, for example, must always be greater than that which employs the spinners; because it not only replaces that capital with its profits, but pays, besides, the wages of weavers; and the profits must always bear some proportion to the capital. (Ibid., Vol. I, p. 45)

Thus the advance made by human labour in converting the product of nature into the manufactured product of nature increases, not the wages of labour, but in part the number of profitable capital investments, and in part the size of every subsequent capital in comparison with the foregoing.

More about the advantages which the capitalist derives from the division of labour, later.

He profits doubly—first, by the division of labour; and secondly, in general, by the advance which human labour makes on the natural product. The greater the human share in a commodity, the greater the profit of dead capital.

In one and the same society the average rates of profit on capital are much more nearly on the same level than the wages of the different sorts of labour. (Ibid., Vol. I, p. 100.) In the different employments of capital, the ordinary rate of profit varies with the certainty or uncertainty of the returns. "The ordinary profit of stock, though it rises with the risk, does not always seem to rise in proportion to it." (Ibid., Vol. I, pp. 99-100.)

It goes without saying that profits also rise if the means of circulation become less expensive or easier available (e.g., paper money).

3. The Rule of Capital over Labour and the Motives of the Capitalist

The consideration of his own private profit is the sole motive which determines the owner of any capital to employ it either in agriculture, in manufactures, or in some particular branch of the wholesale or retail trade. The different quantities of *productive labour* which it may put into motion, and the different values which it may add to the annual produce of the land and labour of his country, according as it is employed in one or other of those different ways, never enter into his thoughts. (Adam Smith, Ibid., Vol. I, p. 335.)

The most useful employment of capital for the capitalist is that which, risks being equal, yields him the greatest profit. This employment is not always the most useful for society; the most useful employment is that which utilises the productive powers of nature. (Say, t. II, pp. 130-31.)

The plans and speculations of the employers of capitals regulate and direct all the most important operations of labour, and *profit* is the end proposed by all those plans and projects. But the rate of profit does not, like rent and wages, rise with the prosperity and fall with the decline of the society. On the contrary, it is naturally low in rich and high in poor countries, and it is always highest in the countries which are going fastest to ruin. The interest of this class, therefore, has not the same connection with the general interest of the society as that of the other two.... The particular interest of the dealers in any particular branch of trade or manufactures is always in some respects different from, and frequently even in sharp opposition to, that of the public. To widen the market and to narrow the sellers' competition is always the interest of the dealer.... This is a class of people whose interest is never exactly the same as that of society, a class of people who have generally an interest to deceive and to oppress the public. (Adam Smith, Ibid., Vol. I, pp. 231-32)

4. The Accumulation of Capitals and the Competition among the Capitalists

The *increase of stock,* which raises wages, tends to lower the capitalists' profit, because of the competition amongst the capitalists. (Adam Smith, Ibid., Vol. I, p. 78.)

If, for example, the capital which is necessary for the grocery trade of a particular town "is divided between two different grocers, their competition will tend to make both of them sell cheaper than if it were in the hands of one only; and if it were divided among twenty, their competition would be just so much the greater, and the chance of their combining together, in order to raise the price, just so much the less." (Adam Smith, Ibid., Vol. I, p. 322.)

Since we already know that monopoly prices are as high as possible, since the interest of the capitalists, even from the point of view commonly held by political economists, stands in hostile opposition to society, and since a rise of profit operates like compound interest on the price of the commodity (Adam Smith, Ibid., Vol. I, pp. 87-88), it follows that the sole defence against the capitalists is *competition,* which according to the evidence of political economy acts beneficently by both raising wages and lowering the prices of commodities to the advantage of the consuming public.

But competition is only possible if capital multiplies, and is held in many hands. The formation of many capital investments is only possible as a result of multilateral accumulation, since capital comes into being only by accumulation; and multilateral accumulation necessarily turns into unilateral accumulation. Competition among capitalists increases the accumulation of capital. Accumulation, where private property prevails, is the *concentration* of capital in the hands of a few, it is in general an inevitable consequence if capital is left to follow its natural course, and it is precisely through competition that the way is cleared for this natural disposition of capital.

We have been told that the profit on capital is in proportion to the size of the capital. A large capital therefore accumulates more quickly than a small capital in proportion to its size, even if we disregard for the time being deliberate competition.

[13]Accordingly, the accumulation of large capital proceeds much more rapidly than that of smaller capital, quite irrespective of competition. But let us follow this process further.

With the increase of capital the profit on capital diminishes, because of competition. The first to suffer, therefore, is the small capitalist.

The increase of capitals and a large number of capital investments presuppose, further, a condition of advancing wealth in the country.

"In a country which had acquired its full complement of riches [...]the ordinary rate of clear profit would be very small, so the usual [market] rate of interest which could be afforded out of it would be so low as to render it impossible for any but the very

---

[13] The preceding page (VII) of the first manuscript does not contain any text relating to the sections "Profit of Capital" and "Rent of Land" (see Note 1).

wealthiest people to live upon the interest of their money. All people of [...] middling fortunes would be obliged to superintend themselves the employment of their own stocks. It would be necessary that almost every man should be a man of business, or engage in some sort of trade." (Adam Smith, Ibid., Vol. I, p. 86)

This is the situation most dear to the heart of political economy.

"The proportion between capital and revenue, therefore, seems everywhere to regulate the proportion between industry and idleness; wherever capital predominates, industry prevails; wherever revenue, idleness." (Adam Smith, Ibid., Vol. I, p. 301.)

What about the employment of capital, then, in this condition of increased competition?

"As stock increases, the quantity of stock to be lent at interest grows gradually greater and greater. As the quantity of stock to be lent at interest increases, the interest ... diminishes (i) because the market price of things commonly diminishes as their quantity increases. ... and (ii) because with *the increase of capitals* in any country, "it becomes gradually more and more difficult to find within the country a profitable method of employing any new capital. There arises in consequence a competition between different capitals, the owner of one endeavouring to get possession of that employment which is occupied by another. But upon most occasions he can hope to jostle that other out of this employment by no other means but by dealing upon more reasonable terms. He must not only sell what he deals in somewhat cheaper, but in order to get it to sell, he must sometimes, too, buy it dearer. The demand for productive labour, by the increase of the funds which are destined for maintaining it, grows every day greater and greater. Labourers easily find employment, but the owners of capitals find it difficult to get labourers to employ. Their competition raises the wages of labour and sinks the profits of stock." (Adam Smith, Ibid., Vol. I, p. 316.)

Thus the small capitalist has the choice: (1) either to consume his capital, since he can no longer live on the interest—and thus cease to be a capitalist; or (2) to set up a business himself, sell his commodity cheaper, buy dearer than the wealthier capitalist, and pay higher wages—thus ruining himself, the market price being already very low as a result of the intense competition presupposed. If, however, the big capitalist wants to squeeze out the smaller capitalist, he has all the advantages over him which the capitalist has as a capitalist over the worker. The larger size of his capital compensates him for the smaller profits, and he can even bear temporary losses until the smaller capitalist is ruined and he finds himself freed from this competition. In this way, he accumulates the small capitalist's profits.
Furthermore: the big capitalist always buys cheaper than the small one, because he buys bigger quantities. He can therefore well afford to sell cheaper.
But if a fall in the rate of interest turns the middle capitalists from rentiers into businessmen, the increase in business capital and the resulting smaller profit produce conversely a fall in the rate of interest.

"When the profits which can be made by the use of a capital are diminished the price which can be paid for the use of it [...] must necessarily be diminished with them."

(Adam Smith, *loc. cit.*, Vol. I, p. 316)

"As riches, improvement, and population have increased, interest has declined," and consequently the profits of capitalists, "after these [profits] are diminished, stock may not only continue to increase, but to increase much faster than before. [...] A great stock though with small profits, generally increases faster than a small stock with great profits. Money, says the proverb, makes money." (Ibid., Vol. I, p. 83.)

When, therefore, this large capital is opposed by small capitals with small profits, as it is under the presupposed condition of intense competition, it crushes them completely. The necessary result of this competition is a general deterioration of commodities, adulteration, fake production and universal poisoning, evident in large towns.

An important circumstance in the competition of large and small capital is, furthermore, the relation between *fixed capital* and *circulating capital*.

Circulating capital is a capital which is "employed in raising" provisions, "manufacturing, or purchasing goods, and selling them again. [...] The capital employed in this manner yields no revenue or profit to its employer, while it either remains in his possession, or continues in the same shape. [...] His capital is continually going from him in one shape, and returning to him in another, and it is only by means of such circulation, or successive exchanges" and transformations "that it can yield him any profit." Fixed capital consists of capital invested "in the improvement of land, in the purchase of useful machines and instruments of trade, or in such-like things." (Adam Smith, Ibid., Vol. I, pp. 243-44)

"Every saving in the expense of supporting the fixed capital is an improvement of the net revenue of the society. The whole capital of the undertaker of every work is necessarily divided between his fixed and his circulating capital. While his whole capital remains the same, the smaller the one part, the greater must necessarily be the other. It is the circulating capital [Marx uses the French terms *capital fixé* and *capital circulant.—* Ed.] which furnishes the materials and wages of labour, and puts industry into motion. Every saving, therefore, in the expense of maintaining the fixed capital, which does not diminish the productive powers of labour, must increase the fund which puts industry into motion." (Adam Smith, Ibid., Vol. I, p. 257.)

It is clear from the outset that the relation of fixed capital and circulating capital is much more favourable to the big capitalist than to the smaller capitalist. The extra fixed capital required by a very big banker as against a very small one is insignificant. Their fixed capital amounts to nothing more than the office. The equipment of the bigger landowner does not increase in proportion to the size of his estate. Similarly, the credit which a big capitalist enjoys compared with a smaller one means for him all the greater saving in fixed capital—that is, in the amount of ready money he must always have at hand. Finally, it is obvious that where industrial labour has reached a high level, and where therefore almost all manual labour has become factory labour, the entire capital of a small capitalist does not suffice to provide him even with the necessary fixed capital. *As is well known, large-scale cultivation usually provides employment only for a small number of hands.* [Note by Marx in French]

It is generally true that the accumulation of large capital is also *accompanied* by a proportional concentration and simplification of fixed capital, as compared to the smaller capitalists. The big capitalist introduces for himself some kind of organisation of the instruments of labour.

"Similarly, in the sphere of industry every manufactory and mill is already a comprehensive combination of a large material fortune with numerous and varied intellectual capacities and technical skills serving the common purpose of production.... Where legislation preserves landed property in large units, the surplus of a growing population flocks into trades, and it is therefore as in Great Britain in the field of industry, principally, that proletarians aggregate in great numbers. Where, however, the law permits the continuous division of the land, the number of small. debt-encumbered proprietors increases, as in France; and the continuing process of fragmentation throws them into the class of the needy and the discontented. When eventually this fragmentation and indebtedness reaches a higher degree still, big landed property once more swallows up small property, just as large-scale industry destroys small industry. And as larger estates are formed again, large numbers of propertyless workers not required for the cultivation of the soil are again driven into industry." (Schulz, *Bewegung der Production*, pp. 58, 59.)

"Commodities of the same kind change in character as a result of changes in the method of production, and especially as a result of the use of machinery. Only by the exclusion of human power has it become possible to spin from a pound of cotton worth 3 shillings and 8 pence 350 hanks of a total length of 167 English miles (i.e., 36 German miles), and of a commercial value of 25 guineas." (Ibid., p. 62.)

"On the average the prices of cotton-goods have decreased in England during the past 45 years by eleven-twelfths, and according to Marshall's calculations the same amount of manufactured goods for which 16 shillings was still paid in 1814 is now supplied at 1 shilling and 10 pence. The greater cheapness of industrial products expands both consumption at home and the market abroad, and because of this the number of workers in cotton has not only not fallen in Great Britain after the introduction of machines but has risen from forty thousand to one and a half million. As to the earnings of industrial entrepreneurs and workers; the growing competition between the factory owners has resulted in their profits necessarily falling relative to the amount of products supplied by them. In the years 1820-33 the Manchester manufacturer's gross profit on a piece of calico fell from four shillings 1 1/3 pence to one shilling 9 pence. But to make up for this loss, the volume of manufacture has been correspondingly increased. The consequence of this is that separate branches of industry experience over-production to some extent, that frequent bankruptcies occur causing property to fluctuate and vacillate unstably within the class of capitalists and masters of labour, thus throwing into the proletariat some of those who have been ruined economically; and that, frequently and suddenly, close-downs or cuts in employment become necessary, the painful effects of which are always bitterly felt by the class of wage-labourers." (Ibid., p. 63.)

"To hire out one's labour is to begin one's enslavement. To hire out the materials of labour is to establish one's freedom.... Labour is man; the materials, on the other hand, contain nothing human." (Pecqueur, *Théorie sociale, etc.*)

"The material element, which is quite incapable of creating wealth without the other element. labour, acquires the magical virtue of being fertile for them [who own this material element] as if by their own action they had placed there this indispensable element." (Ibid.)

"Supposing that the daily labour of a worker brings him on the average 400 francs a year and that this sum suffices for every adult to live some sort of crude life, then any proprietor receiving 2,000 francs in interest or rent, from a farm, a house, etc., compels indirectly five men to work for him; an income of 100,000 francs represents the labour of 250 men, and that of 1,000,000 francs the labour of 2,500 individuals (hence, 300 million [Louis Philippe] therefore the labour of 750,000 workers)." (Ibid., pp. 412-13.)

"The human law has given owners the right to use and to abuse—that is to say, the right to do what they will with the materials of labour.... They are in no way obliged by law to provide work for the propertyless when required and at all times, or to pay them always an adequate wage, etc. (loc. cit., p. 413.) "Complete freedom concerning the nature, the quantity, the quality and the expediency of production; concerning the use and the disposal of wealth; and full command over the materials of all labour. Everyone is free to exchange what belongs to him as he thinks fit, without considering anything other than his own interest as an individual" (Ibid. p. 413.)

"Competition is merely the expression of the freedom to exchange, which itself is the immediate and logical consequence of the individual's right to use and abuse all the instruments of production. The right to use and abuse, freedom of exchange, and arbitrary competition—these three economic moments, which form one unit, entail the following consequences; each produces what he wishes, as he wishes, when he wishes, where he wishes, produces well or produces badly, produces too much or not enough, too soon or too late, at too high a price or too low a price; none knows whether he will sell, to whom he will sell, how he will sell, when he will sell, where he will sell. And it is the same with regard to purchases. The producer is ignorant of needs and resources, of demand and supply. He sells when he wishes, when he can, where he wishes, to whom he wishes, at the price he wishes. And he buys in the same way. In all this he is ever the plaything of chance, the slave of the law of the strongest, of the least harassed, of the richest.... Whilst at one place there is scarcity, at another there is glut and waste. Whilst one producer sells a lot or at a very high price, and at an enormous profit, the other sells nothing or sells at a loss.... The supply does not know the demand, and the demand does not know the supply. You produce, trusting to a taste, a fashion, which prevails amongst the consuming public. But by the time you are ready to deliver the commodity, the whim has already passed and has settled on some other kind of product.... The inevitable consequences: bankruptcies occurring constantly and universally; miscalculations, sudden ruin and unexpected fortunes, commercial crises, stoppages, periodic gluts or shortages; instability and depreciation of wages and profits, the loss or enormous waste of wealth, time and effort in the arena of fierce competition." (Ibid., pp. 414-16.)

Ricardo in his book [*On the Principles of Political Economy and Taxation*] (rent of land): Nations are merely production-shops; man is a machine for consuming and producing; human life is a kind of capital; economic laws blindly rule the world. For Ricardo men are nothing, the product everything. In the 26th chapter of the French translation it says:

"To an individual with a capital of £20,000 whose profits were £2,000 per annum, it would be a matter quite indifferent whether his capital would employ a hundred or a thousand men.... Is not the real interest of the nation similar? Provided its net real income, its rent and profits be the same, it is of no importance whether the nation consists of ten or twelve millions of inhabitants."—[t. II, pp. 194, 195.] "In fact, says M. Sismondi ([*Nouveaux principes diconomie politique,*] t. II, p. 331), nothing remains to be desired but that the King, living quite alone on the island, should by continuously turning a crank cause automatons to do all the work of England."[14]

"The master who buys the worker's labour at such a low price that it scarcely suffices for the worker's most pressing needs is responsible neither for the inadequacy of the wage nor for the excessive duration of the labour: he himself has to submit to the law which he imposes.... Poverty is not so much caused by men as by the power of things." (Buret, Ibid., p. 82.)

"The inhabitants of many different parts of Great Britain have not capital sufficient to improve and cultivate all their lands. The wool of the southern counties of Scotland is, a great part of it, after a long land carriage through very bad roads, manufactured in Yorkshire, for want of capital to manufacture it at home. There are many little manufacturing towns in Great Britain, of which the inhabitants have not capital sufficient to transport the produce of their own industry to those distant markets where there is demand and consumption for it. If there are any merchants among them, they are properly only the agents of wealthier merchants who reside in some of the greater commercial cities." (Adam Smith, *Wealth of Nations*, Vol. I, pp. 326-27.)

"The annual produce of the land and labour of any nation can be increased in its value by no other means but by increasing either *the number of its productive labourers*, or the *productive power of those labourers* who had before been employed.... In either case an additional capital is almost always required." (Adam Smith, Ibid., Vol. I, pp. 306-07.)

"As the *accumulation* of stock must, in the nature of things, be previous to the division of labour, so labour can be more and more subdivided in proportion only as stock is previously more and more accumulated. The quantity of materials which the same number of people can work up, increases in a great proportion as labour comes to be more and more subdivided; and as the operations of each workman are gradually reduced to a greater degree of simplicity, a variety of new machines come to be invented for facilitating and abridging those operations. As the division of labour advances, therefore, in order to give constant employment to an equal number of workmen, an equal stock of provisions, and a greater stock of materials and tools than what would have been necessary in a ruder state of things, must be accumulated beforehand. But the number of workmen in every branch of business generally increases with the division of labour in that branch, or rather it is the increase of their number which enables them to class and subdivide themselves in this manner." (Adam Smith, Ibid., Vol. I, pp. 241-42.)

"As the accumulation of stock is previously necessary for carrying on this great improvement in the productive powers of labour, so that accumulation naturally leads to this improvement. The person who employs his stock in maintaining labour, necessarily wishes to employ it in such a manner as to produce as great a quantity of work as possible. He endeavours, therefore, both to make among his workmen the most proper distribution of employment, and to furnish them with the best machines which he can either invent or afford to purchase. His abilities in both these respects are generally in proportion to the extent of his stock, or to the number of people whom it can employ. The quantity of industry, therefore, not only increases in every country with the increase *of the stock* which employs it, but, in consequence of that increase, the same quantity of industry produces a much greater quantity of work." (Adam Smith, Ibid., Vol. I, p. 242.)

---

[14] The whole paragraph, including the quotation from Ricardo's book in the French translation by Francisco Solano Constancio: *Des principes de l'economie politique, et de l'impôt*, 2-e éd., Paris, 1835, T. II, pp. 194-95 (see the corresponding English edition *On the Principles of Political Economy, and Taxation*, London, 1817), and from Sismondi's *Nouveaux principes d'économie politique...*, Paris, 1819, T. II., p. 331, is an excerpt from Eugéne Buret's book *De la misère des classes laborieuses en Angleterre et en France....* Paris, 1840, T. I, pp. 6-7, note.

Hence *over-production*.

"More comprehensive combinations of productive forces ... in industry and trade by uniting more numerous and more diverse human and natural powers in larger-scale enterprises. Already here and there, closer association of the chief branches of production. Thus, big manufacturers will try to acquire also large estates in order to become independent of others for at least a part of the raw materials required for their industry; or they will go into trade in conjunction with their industrial enterprises, not only to sell their own manufactures, but also to purchase other kinds of products and to sell these to their workers. In England, where a single factory owner sometimes employs ten to twelve thousand workers ... it is already not uncommon to find such combinations of various branches of production controlled by one brain, such smaller states or provinces within the state. Thus, the mine owners in the Birmingham area have recently taken over the *whole* process of iron production, which was previously distributed among various entrepreneurs and owners, (See "*Der bergmännische Distrikt bei Birmingham*," *Deutsche Vierteljahr-Schrift* No. 3, 1838.) Finally in the large joint-stock enterprises which have become so numerous, we see far-reaching combinations of the financial resources of many participants with the scientific and technical knowledge and skills of others to whom the carrying-out of the work is handed over. The capitalists are thereby enabled to apply their savings in more diverse ways and perhaps even to employ them simultaneously in agriculture, industry and commerce. As a consequence their interest becomes more comprehensive, and the contradictions between agricultural, industrial, and commercial interests are reduced and disappear. But this increased possibility of applying capital profitably in the most diverse ways cannot but intensify the antagonism between the propertied and the non-propertied classes." (Schulz, Ibid., pp. 40-41.)

The enormous profit which the landlords of houses make out of poverty. House rent stands in inverse proportion to industrial poverty.

So does the interest obtained from the vices of the ruined proletarians. (Prostitution, drunkenness, pawnbroking.)

The accumulation of capital increases and the competition between capitalists decreases, when capital and landed property are united in the same hand, also when capital is enabled by its size to combine different branches of production.

Indifference towards men. Smith's twenty lottery-tickets.[15]

Say's net and gross revenue.

RENT OF LAND

Landlords' right has its origin in robbery. (Say, t. 1, p. 136, footnote.) The landlords, like all other men, love to reap where they never sowed, and demand a rent even for the natural produce of the earth. (Adam Smith, Ibid., Vol. I, p. 44.)

"The rent of land, it may be thought, is frequently no more than a reasonable profit or interest for the stock laid out by the landlord upon its improvement. This, no doubt, may be partly the case upon some occasions.... The landlord demands" (1) "a rent even for unimproved land, and the supposed interest or profit upon the expense of improvement is generally an addition to this original rent." (2) "Those improvements, besides, are not

---

[15] The allusion is to the following passage: "In a perfectly fair lottery, those who draw the prizes ought to gain all that is lost by those who draw the blanks. In a profession where twenty fail for one that succeeds, that one ought to gain all that should have been gained by the unsuccessful twenty." (Smith, *Wealth of Nations*, Vol. 1, Bk. 1, p. 94.)

always made by the stock of the landlord, but sometimes by that of the tenant. When the lease comes to be renewed, however, the landlord commonly demands the same augmentation of rent as if they had been all made by his own." (3) "He sometimes demands rent for what is altogether incapable of human improvement." (Adam Smith, Ibid., Vol. I, p. 131)

Smith cites as an instance of the last case kelp, a species of seaweed, which, when burnt, yields an alkaline salt, useful for making glass, soap, etc. It grows in several parts of Great Britain, particularly in Scotland, upon such rocks only as lie within the high-water mark, which are twice every day covered with the sea, and of which the produce, therefore, was never augmented by human industry. The landlord, however, whose estate is bounded by a kelp shore of this kind, demands a rent for it as much as for his corn fields. The sea in the neighborhood of the Islands of Shetland is more than commonly abundant in fish, which make a great part of the subsistence of their inhabitants. But in order to profit by the produce of the water they must have a habitation upon the neighboring land. The rent of the landlord is in proportion, not to what the farmer can make by the land, but to what he can make both by the land and by the water." (Adam Smith, Ibid., Vol. I, p. 131)

"This rent may be considered as the produce of those *powers of nature*, the use of which the landlord lends to the farmer. It is greater or smaller according to the supposed extent of those powers, or in other words, according to the supposed natural or improved fertility of the land. It is the work of nature which remains after deducting or compensating everything which can be regarded as the work of man." (Adam Smith, Ibid., Vol. I, pp. 324-25)

"The *rent of land*, therefore, considered as the price paid for the use of the land, is naturally a *monopoly price*. It is not at all proportioned to what the landlord may have laid out upon the improvement of the land, or to what he can afford to take; but to what the farmer can afford to give." (Adam Smith, Ibid., p. 131)

Of the three original classes, that of the landlords is the one "whose revenue costs them neither labour nor care, but comes to them, as it were, of its own accord, and independent of any plan or project of their own." (Adam Smith, Ibid., Vol. I, p. 230)

We have already learnt that the size of the rent depends on the degree of *fertility* of the land.

Another factor in its determination is *situation*.

"The rent of land not only varies with its *fertility*, whatever be its produce, but with its *situation* whatever be its fertility." (Adam Smith, Ibid., Vol. I, p. 133.)

"The produce of land, mines, and fisheries, when their natural fertility is equal, is in proportion to the extent and proper application of the capitals employed about them. When the capitals are equal and equally well applied, it is in proportion to their natural fertility." (Ibid., Vol. I, p. 249.)

These propositions of Smith are important, because, given equal costs of production and capital of equal size, they reduce the rent of land to the greater or lesser fertility of the soil. Thereby showing clearly the perversion of concepts in political economy, which turns the fertility of the land into an attribute of the landlord.

Now, however, let us consider the rent of land as it is formed in real life.

The rent of land is established as a result of *the struggle between tenant and landlord.* We find that the hostile antagonism of interests, the struggle, the war is recognized throughout political economy as the basis of social organization.

Let us see now what the relations are between landlord and tenant.

"In adjusting the terms of the lease, the landlord endeavors to leave him no greater share of the produce than what is sufficient to keep up the stock from which he furnishes the seed, pays the labour, and purchases and maintains the cattle and other instruments of husbandry, together with the ordinary profits of farming stock in the neighbourhood. This is evidently the smallest share with which the tenant can content himself without being a loser, and the landlord seldom means to leave him any more. Whatever part of the produce, or, what is the same thing, whatever part of its price is over and above this share, he naturally endeavors to reserve to himself as the rent of his land, which is evidently the highest the tenant can afford to pay in the actual circumstances of the land. [...] This portion, however, may still be considered as the natural rent of land, or the rent for which it is naturally meant that land should for the most part be let." (Adam Smith, Ibid., Vol. I, pp. 130-31.)

"The landlords," says Say, "operate a certain kind of monopoly against the tenants. The demand for their commodity, site and soil, can go on expanding indefinitely; but there is only a given, limited amount of their commodity.... The bargain struck between landlord and tenant is always advantageous to the former in the greatest possible degree.... Besides the advantage he derives from the nature of the case, he derives a further advantage from his position, his larger fortune and greater credit and standing. But the first by itself suffices to enable him and him *alone* to profit from the favorable circumstances of the land. The opening of a canal, or a road; the increase of population and of the prosperity of a district, always raises the rent.... Indeed, the tenant himself may improve the ground at his own expense; but he only derives the profit from this capital for the duration of his lease, with the expiry of which it remains with the proprietor of the land; henceforth it is the latter who reaps the interest thereon, without having made the outlay, for there is now a proportionate increase in the rent." (Say, t. II., pp. 142-43.)

"Rent, considered as the price paid for the use of land, is naturally the highest which the tenant can afford to pay in the actual circumstances of the land." (Adam Smith, Ibid., Vol. I, p. 130)

"The rent of an estate above ground commonly amounts to what is supposed to be a third of the gross produce; and it is generally a rent certain and independent of the occasional variations in the crop." (Adam Smith, Ibid., Vol. I, p. 153.) This rent "is seldom less than a fourth ... of the whole produce." (Ibid., Vol. I, p. 325.)

Rent cannot be paid on all commodities. For instance, in many districts no rent is paid for stones.

"Such parts only of the produce of land can commonly be brought to market of which the ordinary price is sufficient to replace the stock which must be employed in bringing them thither, together with its ordinary profits. If the ordinary price is more than this, the surplus part of it will naturally go to the rent of the land. If it is not more, though the commodity may be brought to market, it can afford no rent to the landlord. Whether the price is or is not more depends upon the demand." (Adam Smith, Ibid., Vol. I, p. 132.)

"Rent, it is to be observed, therefore, enters into the composition of the *price of commodities* in a *different way* from wages and profit. *High or low wages and profit* are the *causes* of high or low price; high or low rent is the *effect* of it." (Adam Smith, *loc. cit.*, Vol. I, p. 132)

Food belongs to the *products* which always yield a *rent*.

"As men, like all other animals, naturally multiply in proportion to the means of their subsistence, food is always, more or less, in demand. It can always purchase or command a greater or smaller quantity of labour, and somebody can always be found who is willing to do something in order to obtain it. The quantity of labour, indeed, which it can purchase is not always *equal* to what it could maintain, if managed in the most economical manner, on account of the high wages which are sometimes given to labour. But it can always purchase such a quantity of labour as it can maintain, according to the rate at which the sort of labour is commonly maintained in the neighborhood.

"But land, in almost any situation, produces a greater quantity of food than what is sufficient to maintain all the labour necessary for bringing it to market in the most liberal way in which that labour is ever maintained. [...] The surplus, too, is always more than sufficient to replace the stock which employed that labour, together with its profits. Something, therefore, always remains for a rent to the landlord." (Adam Smith, Ibid., Vol. I, pp. 132-33.)

"Food is in this manner not only the original source of rent, but every other part of the produce of land which afterwards affords rent derives that part of its value from the improvement of the powers of labour in producing food by means of the improvement and cultivation of land." (Adam Smith, Ibid., Vol. I, p. 150.)

"Human food seems to be the only produce of land which always and necessarily affords some rent to the landlord." (Ibid., Vol. I, p. 147.)

"Countries are populous not in proportion to the number of people whom their produce can clothe and lodge, but in proportion to that of those whom it can feed." (Adam Smith, Ibid., Vol. I, p. 149.)

"After food, clothing and lodging are the two great wants of mankind." They usually yield a rent, but not inevitably. (Ibid., Vol. I, p. 147.)

[16]Let us now see how the landlord exploits everything from which society benefits.
(1) The rent of land increases with population. (Adam Smith, Ibid., Vol. I, p. 146.)
(2) We have already learnt from Say how the rent of land increases with railways, etc., with the improvement, safety, and multiplication of the means of communication.

(3) "Every improvement in the circumstances of the society tends either *directly or indirectly* to raise the real rent of land, to increase the real wealth of the landlord, his power of purchasing the labour, or the produce of the labour of other people...The extension of improvement and cultivation tends to raise it directly. The landlord's share of the produce necessarily increases with the increase of the produce. That rise in the real price of those parts of the rude produce of land,... the rise in the price of cattle, for example, tends too to raise the rent of land directly, and in a still greater proportion. The real value of the landlord's share, his real command of the labour of other people, not only rises with the real value of the produce, but the proportion of his share to the whole produce rises with it. That produce, after the rise in its real price, requires no more labour

---

[16] See Note 12.

to collect it than before. A smaller proportion of it will, therefore, be sufficient to replace, with the ordinary profit, the stock which employs that labour. A greater proportion of it must, consequently, belong to the landlord." (Adam Smith, Ibid., Vol. I, pp. 228-29.)

The greater demand for raw produce, and therefore the rise in value, may in part result from the increase of population and from the increase of their needs. But every new invention, every new application in manufacture of a previously unused or little-used raw material, augments rent. Thus, for example, there was a tremendous rise in the rent of coal mines with the advent of the railways, steamships, etc.

Besides this advantage which the landlord derives from manufacture, discoveries, and labour, there is yet another, as we shall presently see.

(4) "All those improvements in the productive powers of labour, which tend directly to reduce the real price of manufactures, tend indirectly to raise the real rent of land. The landlord exchanges that part of his rude produce, which is over and above his own consumption, or what comes to the same thing, the price of that part of it, for manufactured produce. Whatever reduces the real price of the latter, raises that of the former. An equal quantity of the former becomes thereby equivalent to a greater quantity of the latter; and the landlord is enabled to purchase a greater quantity of the conveniences, ornaments, or luxuries, which he has occasion for." (Adam Smith, Ibid., Vol. I, p. 229.)

But it is silly to conclude, as Smith does, that since the landlord exploits every benefit which comes to society the interest of the landlord is always identical with that of society. (Ibid., Vol. I, p. 230.) In the economic system, under the rule of private property, the interest which an individual has in society is in precisely inverse proportion to the interest society has in him—just as the interest of the usurer in the spendthrift is by no means identical with the interest of the spendthrift.

We shall mention only in passing the landlord's obsession with monopoly directed against the landed property of foreign countries, from which the Corn Laws,[17] for instance, originate. Likewise, we shall here pass over medieval serfdom, the slavery in the colonies, and the miserable condition of the country folk, the day-labourers, in Great Britain. Let us confine ourselves to the propositions of political economy itself.

(1) The landlord being interested in the welfare of society means, according to the principles of political economy, that he is interested in the growth of its population and manufacture, in the expansion of its needs—in short, in the increase of wealth; and this increase of wealth is, as we have already seen, identical with the increase of poverty and slavery. The relation between increasing house rent and increasing poverty is an example of the landlord's interest in society, for the ground rent, the interest obtained from the

---

[17] The Corn Laws—a series of laws in England (the first of which dated back to the 15th century) which imposed high duties on imported corn with the aim of maintaining high prices on it on the home market. In the first third of the 19th century several laws were passed (in 1815, 1822 and so on) changing the conditions of corn imports, and in 1828 a sliding scale was introduced, which raised import duties on corn while lowering prices on the home market and, on the contrary, lowered import duties while raising prices.

In 1838 the Manchester factory owners Cobden and Bright founded the Anti-Corn Law League, which widely exploited the popular discontent at rising corn prices. While agitating for the abolition of the corn duties and demanding complete freedom of trade, the League strove to weaken the economic and political positions of the landed aristocracy and to lower workers' wages.

The struggle between the industrial bourgeoisie and the landed aristocracy over the Corn Laws ended in their repeal in 1846.

land on which the house stands, goes up with the rent of the house.

(2) According to the political economists themselves, the landlord's interest is inimically opposed to the interest of the tenant farmer—and thus already to a significant section of society.

(3) As the landlord can demand all the more rent from the tenant farmer the less wages the farmer pays, and as the farmer forces down wages all the lower the more rent the landlord demands, it follows that the interest of the landlord is just as hostile to that of the farm workers as is that of the manufacturers to their workers. He likewise forces down wages to the minimum.

(4) Since a real reduction in the price of manufactured products raises the rent of land, the landowner has a direct interest in lowering the wages of industrial workers, in competition amongst the capitalists, in over-production, in all the misery associated with industrial production.

(5) While, thus, the landlord's interest, far from being identical with the interest of society, stands inimically opposed to the interest of tenant farmers, farm labourers, factory workers and capitalists, on the other hand, the interest of one landlord is not even identical with that of another, on account of the competition which we will now consider.

In general the relationship of large and small landed property is like that of big and small capital. But in addition, there are special circumstances which lead inevitably to the accumulation of large landed property and to the absorption of small property by it.

(1) Nowhere does the relative number of workers and implements decrease more with increases in the size of the stock than in landed property. Likewise, the possibility of all-round exploitation, of economizing production costs, and of effective division of labour, increases nowhere more with the size of the stock than in landed property. However small a field may be, it requires for its working a certain irreducible minimum of implements (plough, saw, etc.), whilst the size of a piece of landed property can be reduced far below this minimum.

(2) Big landed property accumulates to itself the interest on the capital which the tenant farmer has employed to improve the land. Small landed property has to employ its own capital, and therefore does not get this profit at all.

(3) While every social improvement benefits the big estate, it harms small property, because it increases its need for ready cash.

(4) Two important laws concerning this competition remain to be considered:

(α) The rent of the cultivated land, of which the produce is human food, regulates the rent of the greater part of other cultivated land. (Adam Smith, Ibid., Vol. I, p. 144.)

Ultimately, only the big estate can produce such food as cattle, etc. Therefore it regulates the rent of other land and can force it down to a minimum.

The small landed proprietor working on his own land stands then to the big landowner in the same relation as an artisan possessing his *own* tool to the factory owner. Small property in land has become a mere instrument of labour. [18] Rent entirely disappears for the small proprietor; there remains to him at the most the interest on his capital, and his wages. For rent can be driven down by competition till it is nothing more than the interest on capital not invested by the proprietor.

(β) In addition, we have already learnt that with equal fertility and equally efficient exploitation of lands, mines and fisheries, the produce is proportionate to the size of the

---

[18] Pages XIII to XV are divided into two columns and not three like the other pages of the first manuscript; they contain no text relating to the section "Rent of Land." On page XVI, which also has two columns, this text is in the first column, while on the following pages it is in the second.

capital. Hence the victory of the big landowner. Similarly, where equal capitals are employed the product is proportionate to the fertility. Hence, where capitals are equal, victory goes to the proprietor of the more fertile soil.

(γ) "A mine of any kind may be said to be either fertile or barren, according as the quantity of mineral which can be brought from it by a certain quantity of labour is greater or less than what can be brought by an equal quantity from the greater part of other mines of the same kind." (Adam Smith, Ibid., Vol. I, p. 151.)

"The most fertile coal-mine, too, regulates the price of coal at all the other mines in its neighborhood. Both the proprietor and the undertaker of the work find, the one that he can get a greater rent, the other that he can get a greater profit, by somewhat underselling all their neighbors. Their neighbors are soon obliged to sell at the same price, though they cannot so well afford it, and though it always diminishes, and sometimes takes away altogether both their rent and their profit. Some works are abandoned altogether; others can afford no rent, and can be wrought only by the proprietor." (Adam Smith, Ibid., Vol. I, pp. 152-53.)

"After the discovery of the mines of Peru, the silver mines of Europe were, the greater part of them, abandoned.... This was the case, too, with the mines of Cuba and St. Domingo, and even with the ancient mines of Peru, after the discovery of those of Potosi." (Ibid., Vol. I, p. 154.)

What Smith here says of mines applies more or less to landed property generally:

(δ) "The ordinary market price of land, it is to be observed, depends everywhere upon the ordinary market rate of interest.... If the rent of land should fall short of the interest of money by a greater difference, nobody would buy land, which would soon reduce its ordinary price. On the contrary, if the advantages should much more than compensate the difference, everybody would buy land, which again would soon raise its ordinary price." (Ibid., Vol. I, p. 320.)

From this relation of rent of land to interest on money it follows that rent must fall more and more, so that eventually only the wealthiest people can live on rent. Hence the ever greater competition between landowners who do not lease their land to tenants. Ruin of some of these; further accumulation of large landed property.

This competition has the further consequence that a large part of landed property falls into the hands of the capitalists and that capitalists thus become simultaneously landowners, just as the smaller landowners are on the whole already nothing more than capitalists. Similarly, a section of large landowners become at the same time industrialists.

The final consequence is thus the abolition of the distinction between capitalist and landowner, so that there remain altogether only two classes of the population—the working class and the class of capitalists. This huckstering with landed property, the transformation of landed property into a commodity, constitutes the final overthrow of the old and the final establishment of the money aristocracy.

(1) We will not join in the sentimental tears wept over this by romanticism. Romanticism always confuses the shamefulness of *huckstering the land* with the perfectly rational consequence, inevitable and desirable within the realm of private property, of the *huckstering of private property* in land. In the first place, feudal landed property is already by its very nature huckstered land—the earth which is estranged from

man and hence confronts him in the shape of a few great lords.

The domination of the land as an alien power over men is already inherent in feudal landed property. The serf is the adjunct of the land. Likewise, the lord of an entailed estate, the first-born son, belongs to the land. It inherits him. Indeed, the dominion of private property begins with property in land—that is its basis. But in feudal landed property the lord at least *appears* as the king of the estate. Similarly, there still exists the semblance of a more intimate connection between the proprietor and the land than that of mere *material* wealth. The estate is individualized with its lord: it has his rank, is baronial or ducal with him, has his privileges, his jurisdiction, his political position, etc. It appears as the inorganic body of its lord. Hence the proverb *nulle terre sans maître*,[19] which expresses the fusion of nobility and landed property. Similarly, the rule of landed property does not appear directly as the rule of mere capital. For those belonging to it, the estate is more like their fatherland. It is a constricted sort of nationality.

In the same way, feudal landed property gives its name to its lord, as does a kingdom to its king. His family history, the history of his house, etc.—all this individualizes the estate for him and makes it literally his house, personifies it. Similarly those working on the estate have not the position *of day-labourers*; but they are in part themselves his property, as are serfs; and in part they are bound to him by ties of respect, allegiance, and duty. His relation to them is therefore directly political, and has likewise a human, intimate side. Customs, character, etc., vary from one estate to another and seem to be one with the land to which they belong; whereas later, it is only his purse and not his character, his individuality, which connects a man with an estate. Finally, the feudal lord does not try to extract the utmost advantage from his land. Rather, he consumes what is there and calmly leaves the worry of producing to the serfs and the tenants. Such is *nobility's* relationship to landed property, which casts a romantic glory on its lords.

It is necessary that this appearance be abolished—that landed property, the root of private property, be dragged completely into the movement of private property and that it become a commodity; that the rule of the proprietor appear as the undisguised rule of private property, of capital, freed of all political tincture; that the relationship between proprietor and worker be reduced to the economic relationship of exploiter and exploited; that all ... personal relationship between the proprietor and his property cease, property becoming merely *objective*, material wealth; that the marriage of convenience should take the place of the marriage of honor with the land; and that the land should likewise sink to the status of a commercial value, like man. It is essential that that which is the root of landed property—filthy self-interest—make its appearance, too, in its cynical form. It is essential that the immovable monopoly turn into the mobile and restless monopoly, into competition; and that the idle enjoyment of the products of other people's blood and sweat turn into a bustling commerce in the same commodity. Lastly, it is essential that in this competition landed property, in the form of capital, manifest its dominion over both the working class and the proprietors themselves who are either being ruined or raised by the laws governing the movement of capital. The medieval proverb *nulle terre sans seigneur*[20] is thereby replaced by that other proverb, *l'argent n'a pas de maître*,[21] wherein is expressed the complete domination of dead matter over man.

(2) Concerning the argument of division or non-division of landed property, the following is to be observed.

---

[19] There is no land without its master.—Ed
[20] There is no land without its lord.—Ed
[21] Money knows no master.—Ed

The *division of landed property* negates the *large-scale monopoly* of property in land—abolishes it; but only by *generalizing* this monopoly. It does not abolish the source of monopoly, private property. It attacks the existing form, but not the essence, of monopoly. The consequence is that it falls victim to the laws of private property. For the division of landed property corresponds to the movement of competition in the sphere of industry. In addition to the economic disadvantages of such a dividing-up of the instruments of labour, and the dispersal of labour (to be clearly distinguished from the division of labour: in separated labour the work is not shared out amongst many, but each carries on the same work by himself, it is a multiplication of the same work), this division of land, like that competition in industry, necessarily turns again into accumulation.

Therefore, where the division of landed property takes place, there remains nothing for it but to return to monopoly in a still more malignant form, or to negate, to abolish the division of landed property itself. To do that, however, is not to return to feudal ownership, but to abolish private property in the soil altogether. The first abolition of monopoly is always its generalization, the broadening of its existence. The abolition of monopoly, once it has come to exist in its utmost breadth and inclusiveness, is its total annihilation. Association, applied to land, shares the economic advantage of large-scale landed property, and first brings to realization the original tendency inherent in [land] division, namely, equality. In the same way association also re-establishes, now on a rational basis, no longer mediated by serfdom, overlordship and the silly mysticism of property, the intimate ties of man with the earth, since the earth ceases to be an object of huckstering, and through free labour and free enjoyment becomes once more a true personal property of man. A great advantage of the division of landed property is that the masses, which can no longer resign themselves to servitude, perish through property in a different way than in industry.

As for large landed property, its defenders have always, sophistically, identified the economic advantages offered by large-scale agriculture with large-scale landed property, as if it were not precisely as a result of the abolition of property that this advantage, for one thing, would receive its greatest possible extension, and, for another, only then would be of social benefit. In the same way, they have attacked the huckstering spirit of small landed property, as if large landed property did not contain huckstering latent within it, even in its feudal form—not to speak of the modern English form, which combines the landlord's feudalism with the tenant farmer's huckstering and industry.

Just as large landed property can return the reproach of monopoly leveled against it by partitioned land, since partitioned land is also based on the monopoly of private property, so can partitioned landed property likewise return to large landed property the reproach of partition, since partition also prevails there, though in a rigid and frozen form. Indeed, private property rests altogether on partitioning. Moreover, just as division of the land leads back to large landed property as a form of capital wealth, so must feudal landed property necessarily lead to partitioning or at least fall into the hands of the capitalists, turn and twist as it may.

For large landed property, as in England, drives the overwhelming majority of the population into the arms of industry and reduces its own workers to utter wretchedness. Thus, it engenders and enlarges the power of its enemy, capital, industry, by throwing poor people and an entire activity of the country on to the other side. It makes the majority of the people of the country industrial and thus opponents of large landed property. Where industry has attained to great power, as in England at the present time, it progressively forces from large landed property its monopoly against foreign countries and throws it into competition with landed property abroad. For under the sway of industry landed property could keep its feudal grandeur secure only by means of monopolies against foreign countries, thereby protecting itself against the general laws of trade, which are incompatible with its feudal character. Once thrown into competition, landed property obeys the laws of competition, like every other commodity subjected to competition. It begins thus to fluctuate, to decrease and to increase, to fly from one hand to another; and no law can keep it any longer in a few predestined hands. The immediate consequence is the splitting up of the land amongst many hands, and in any case subjection to the power of industrial capitals.

Finally, large landed property which has been forcibly preserved in this way and which has begotten by its side a tremendous industry leads to crisis even more quickly than the partitioning of land, in comparison with which the power of industry remains constantly of second rank.

Large landed property, as we see in England, has already cast off its feudal character and adopted an industrial character insofar as it is aiming to make as much money as possible. To the owner it yields the utmost possible rent, to the tenant farmer the utmost possible profit on his capital. The workers on the land, in consequence, have already been reduced to the minimum, and the class of tenant farmers already represents within landed property the power of industry and capital. As a result of foreign competition, rent in most cases can no longer form an independent income. A large number of landowners are forced to displace tenant farmers, some of whom in this way … sink into the proletariat. On the other hand, many tenant farmers will take over landed property; for the big proprietors, who with their comfortable incomes have mostly given themselves over to extravagance and for the most part are not competent to conduct large-scale agriculture, often possess neither the capital nor the ability for the exploitation of the land. Hence a section of this class, too, is completely ruined. Eventually wages, which have already been reduced to a minimum, must be reduced yet further, to meet the new competition. This then necessarily leads to revolution.

Landed property had to develop in each of these two ways so as to experience in both its necessary downfall, just as industry both in the form of monopoly and in that of competition had to ruin itself so as to learn to believe in man.

ESTRANGED LABOUR

We have proceeded from the premises of political economy. We have accepted its language and its laws. We presupposed private property, the separation of labor, capital and land, and of wages, profit of capital and rent of land—likewise division of labor, competition, the concept of exchange value, etc. On the basis of political economy itself, in its own words, we have shown that the worker sinks to the level of a commodity and becomes indeed the most wretched of commodities; that the wretchedness of the worker is in inverse proportion to the power and magnitude of his production; that the necessary result of competition is the accumulation of capital in a few hands, and thus the restoration of monopoly in a more terrible form; and that finally the distinction between capitalist and land rentier, like that between the tiller of the soil and the factory worker, disappears and that the whole of society must fall apart into the two classes—*property owners* and propertyless *workers*.

Political economy starts with the fact of private property; it does not explain it to us. It expresses in general, abstract formulas the *material* process through which private property actually passes, and these formulas it then takes for *laws*. It does not *comprehend* these laws—i.e., it does not demonstrate how they arise from the very nature of private property. Political economy throws no light on the cause of the division between labor and capital, and between capital and land. When, for example, it defines the relationship of wages to profit, it takes the interest of the capitalists to be the ultimate cause, i.e., it takes for granted what it is supposed to explain. Similarly, competition comes in everywhere. It is explained from external circumstances. As to how far these external and apparently accidental circumstances are but the expression of a necessary course of development, political economy teaches us nothing. We have seen how exchange itself appears to it as an accidental fact. The only wheels which political economy sets in motion are *greed*, and the *war amongst the greedy—competition*.

Precisely because political economy does not grasp the way the movement is connected, it was possible to oppose, for instance, the doctrine of competition to the doctrine of monopoly, the doctrine of craft freedom to the doctrine of the guild, the doctrine of the division of landed property to the doctrine of the big estate—for competition, freedom of the crafts and the division of landed property were explained and comprehended only as accidental, premeditated and violent consequences of monopoly, of the guild system, and of feudal property, not as their necessary, inevitable and natural consequences.

Now, therefore, we have to grasp the intrinsic connection between private property, greed, the separation of labor, capital and landed property; the connection of exchange and competition, of value and the devaluation of man, of monopoly and competition, etc.—the connection between this whole estrangement and the *money* system.

Do not let us go back to a fictitious primordial condition as the political economist does, when he tries to explain. Such a primordial condition explains nothing; it merely pushes the question away into a grey nebulous distance. The economist assumes in the form of a fact, of an event, what he is supposed to deduce—namely, the necessary relationship between two things—between, for example, division of labor and exchange. Thus the theologian explains the origin of evil by the fall of Man—that is, he assumes as a fact, in historical form, what has to be explained.

We proceed from an *actual* economic fact.

The worker becomes all the poorer the more wealth he produces, the more his production increases in power and size. The worker becomes an ever cheaper commodity the more commodities he creates. The *devaluation* of the world of men is in direct proportion to the *increasing value* of the world of things. Labor produces not only commodities; it produces itself and the worker as a *commodity*—and this at the same rate at which it produces commodities in general.

This fact expresses merely that the object which labor produces—labor's product—confronts it as *something alien*, as a *power independent* of the producer. The product of labor is labor which has been embodied in an object, which has become material: it is the *objectification* of labor. Labor's realization is its objectification. Under these economic conditions this realization of labor appears as *loss of realization* for the workers;[22] objectification as *loss of the object and bondage to it;* appropriation as *estrangement*, as *alienation*.[23]

---

[22] Marx, still using Hegel's terminology and his approach to the unity of the opposites, counterposes the term "Verwirklichung" (realisation) to "Entwirklichung" (loss of realisation).

[23] In this manuscript Marx frequently uses two similar German terms, "*Entäusserung*" and "*Entfremdung*," to express the notion of "alienation." In the present edition the former is generally translated as "alienation," the latter as "estrangement,"

So much does the labor's realization appear as loss of realization that the worker loses realization to the point of starving to death. So much does objectification appear as loss of the object that the worker is robbed of the objects most necessary not only for his life but for his work. Indeed, labor itself becomes an object which he can obtain only with the greatest effort and with the most irregular interruptions. So much does the appropriation of the object appear as estrangement that the more objects the worker produces the less he can possess and the more he falls under the sway of his product, capital.

All these consequences are implied in the statement that the worker is related to the *product of labor* as to an *alien* object. For on this premise it is clear that the more the worker spends himself, the more powerful becomes the alien world of objects which he creates over and against himself, the poorer he himself—his inner world—becomes, the less belongs to him as his own. It is the same in religion. The more man puts into God, the less he retains in himself. The worker puts his life into the object; but now his life no longer belongs to him but to the object. Hence, the greater this activity, the more the worker lacks objects. Whatever the product of his labor is, he is not. Therefore, the greater this product, the less is he himself. The *alienation* of the worker in his product means not only that his labor becomes an object, an *external* existence, but that it exists *outside him*, independently, as something alien to him, and that it becomes a power on its own confronting him. It means that the life which he has conferred on the object confronts him as something hostile and alien.

Let us now look more closely at the *objectification*, at the production of the worker; and in it at the *estrangement*, the loss of the object, of his product.

The worker can create nothing without *nature*, without the *sensuous external world*. It is the material on which his labor is realized, in which it is active, from which, and by means of which it produces.

But just as nature provides labor with [the] *means of life* in the sense that labor cannot *live* without objects on which to operate, on the other hand, it also provides the *means of life* in the more restricted sense, i.e., the means for the physical subsistence of the *worker* himself.

Thus the more the worker by his labor *appropriates* the external world, sensuous nature, the more he deprives himself of the *means of life* in two respects: first, in that the sensuous external world more and more ceases to be an object belonging to his labor—to be his labor's *means of life*; and, second, in that it more and more ceases to be a *means of life* in the immediate sense, means for the physical subsistence of the worker.

In both respects, therefore, the worker becomes a servant of his object, first, in that he receives an *object of labor*, i.e., in that he receives *work*, and, secondly, in that he receives *means of subsistence*. This enables him to exist, first as a worker; and second, as a *physical subject*. The height of this servitude is that it is only as a *worker* that he can maintain himself as a *physical subject* and that it is only as a *physical subject* that he is a worker.

(According to the economic laws the estrangement of the worker in his object is expressed thus: the more the worker produces, the less he has to consume; the more values he creates, the more valueless, the more unworthy he becomes; the better formed his product, the more deformed becomes the worker; the more civilized his object, the more barbarous becomes the worker; the more powerful labor becomes, the more

---

because in the later economic works (*Theories of Surplus-Value*) Marx himself used the word "alienation" as the English equivalent of the term "*Entäusserung.*"

powerless becomes the worker; the more ingenious labor becomes, the less ingenious becomes the worker and the more he becomes nature's slave.)

Political economy conceals the estrangement inherent in the nature of labor by not considering the direct *relationship between the* worker (labor) *and production.* It is true that labor produces for the rich wonderful things—but for the worker it produces privation. It produces palaces—but for the worker, hovels. It produces beauty—but for the worker, deformity. It replaces labor by machines, but it throws one section of the workers back into barbarous types of labor and it turns the other section into a machine. It produces intelligence—but for the worker, stupidity, cretinism.

The direct relationship of labor to its products is the relationship of the worker to the objects of his production. The relationship of the man of means to the objects of production and to production itself is only a *consequence* of this first relationship—and confirms it. We shall consider this other aspect later. When we ask, then, what is the essential relationship of labor we are asking about the relationship of the *worker* to production.

Till now we have been considering the estrangement, the alienation of the worker only in one of its aspects , i.e., *the* worker's *relationship to the products of his labor.* But the estrangement is manifested not only in the result but in the *act of production*, within the *producing activity,* itself. How could the worker come to face the product of his activity as a stranger, were it not that in the very act of production he was estranging himself from himself? The product is after all but the summary of the activity, of production. If then the product of labor is alienation, production itself must be active alienation, the alienation of activity, the activity of alienation. In the estrangement of the object of labor is merely summarized the estrangement, the alienation, in the activity of labor itself.

What, then, constitutes the alienation of labor?

First, the fact that labor is *external* to the worker, i.e., it does not belong to his intrinsic nature; that in his work, therefore, he does not affirm himself but denies himself, does not feel content but unhappy, does not develop freely his physical and mental energy but mortifies his body and ruins his mind. The worker therefore only feels himself outside his work, and in his work feels outside himself. He feels at home when he is not working, and when he is working he does not feel at home. His labor is therefore not voluntary, but coerced; it is *forced labor*. It is therefore not the satisfaction of a need; it is merely a *means* to satisfy needs external to it. Its alien character emerges clearly in the fact that as soon as no physical or other compulsion exists, labor is shunned like the plague. External labor, labor in which man alienates himself, is a labor of self-sacrifice, of mortification. Lastly, the external character of labor for the worker appears in the fact that it is not his own, but someone else's, that it does not belong to him, that in it he belongs, not to himself, but to another. Just as in religion the spontaneous activity of the human imagination, of the human brain and the human heart, operates on the individual independently of him—that is, operates as an alien, divine or diabolical activity—so is the worker's activity not his spontaneous activity. It belongs to another; it is the loss of his self.

As a result, therefore, man (the worker) only feels himself freely active in his animal functions—eating, drinking, procreating, or at most in his dwelling and in dressing-up, etc.; and in his human functions he no longer feels himself to be anything but an animal. What is animal becomes human and what is human becomes animal.

Certainly eating, drinking, procreating, etc., are also genuinely human functions. But taken abstractly, separated from the sphere of all other human activity and turned into sole and ultimate ends, they are animal functions.

We have considered the act of estranging practical human activity, labor, in two of its aspects. (1) The relation of the worker to the *product of labor* as an alien object exercising power over him. This relation is at the same time the relation to the sensuous external world, to the objects of nature, as an alien world inimically opposed to him. (2) The relation of labor to the *act of production* within the *labor* process. This relation is the relation of the worker to his own activity as an alien activity not belonging to him; it is activity as suffering, strength as weakness, begetting as emasculating, the worker's *own* physical and mental energy, his personal life—for what is life but activity?—as an activity which is turned against him, independent of him and not belonging to him. Here we have *self-estrangement,* as previously we had the estrangement of the *thing.*

We have still a third aspect of *estranged labor* to deduce from the two already considered.

Man is a species-being,[24] not only because in practice and in theory he adopts the species (his own as well as those of other things) as his object, but—and this is only another way of expressing it—also because he treats himself as the actual, living species; because he treats himself as a *universal* and therefore a *free* being.

The life of the species, both in man and in animals, consists physically in the fact that man (like the animal) lives on organic nature; and the more universal man (or the animal) is, the more universal is the sphere of inorganic nature on which he lives. Just as plants, animals, stones, air, light, etc., constitute theoretically a part of human consciousness, partly as objects of natural science, partly as objects of art—his spiritual inorganic nature, spiritual nourishment which he must first prepare to make palatable and digestible—so also in the realm of practice they constitute a part of human life and human activity. Physically man lives only on these products of nature, whether they appear in the form of food, heating, clothes, a dwelling, etc. The universality of man appears in practice precisely in the universality which makes all nature his *inorganic* body—both inasmuch as nature is (1) his direct means of life, and (2) the material, the object, and the instrument of his life activity. Nature is man's *inorganic* body—nature, that is, insofar as it is not itself human body. Man *lives* on nature—means that nature is his body, with which he must remain in continuous interchange if he is not to die. That man's physical and spiritual life is linked to nature means simply that nature is linked to itself, for man is a part of nature.

In estranging from man (1) nature, and (2) himself, his own active functions, his life activity, estranged labor estranges the *species* from man. It changes for him the *life of the species* into a means of individual life. First it estranges the life of the species and individual life, and secondly it makes individual life in its abstract form the purpose of the life of the species, likewise in its abstract and estranged form.

For labor, *life activity, productive life* itself, appears to man in the first place merely as a means of satisfying a need—the need to maintain physical existence. Yet the productive life is the life of the species. It is life-engendering life. The whole character of a species, its species-character, is contained in the character of its life activity; and free, conscious activity is man's species-character. Life itself appears only as a *means to life.*

The animal is immediately one with its life activity. It does not distinguish itself from it. It is *its life activity.* Man makes his life activity itself the object of his will and of

---

[24] The term "species-being" (*Gattungswesen*) is derived from Ludwig Feuerbach's philosophy where it is applied to man and mankind as a whole.

his consciousness. He has conscious life activity. It is not a determination with which he directly merges. Conscious life activity distinguishes man immediately from animal life activity. It is just because of this that he is a species-being. Or it is only because he is a species-being that he is a conscious being, i.e., that his own life is an object for him. Only because of that is his activity free activity. Estranged labor reverses the relationship, so that it is just because man is a conscious being that he makes his life activity, his *essential being,* a mere means to his *existence.*

In creating a *world of objects* by his personal activity, in his *work upon* inorganic nature, man proves himself a conscious species-being, i.e., as a being that treats the species as his own essential being, or that treats itself as a species-being. Admittedly animals also produce. They build themselves nests, dwellings, like the bees, beavers, ants, etc. But an animal only produces what it immediately needs for itself or its young. It produces one-sidedly, whilst man produces universally. It produces only under the dominion of immediate physical need, whilst man produces even when he is free from physical need and only truly produces in freedom therefrom. An animal produces only itself, whilst man reproduces the whole of nature. An animal's product belongs immediately to its physical body, whilst man freely confronts his product. An animal forms only in accordance with the standard and the need of the species to which it belongs, whilst man knows how to produce in accordance with the standard of every species, and knows how to apply everywhere the inherent standard to the object. Man therefore also forms objects in accordance with the laws of beauty.

It is just in his work upon the objective world, therefore, that man really proves himself to be a *species-being.* This production is his active species-life. Through this production, nature appears as *his* work and his reality. The object of labor is, therefore, the *objectification of man's species-life:* for he duplicates himself not only, as in consciousness, intellectually, but also actively, in reality, and therefore he sees himself in a world that he has created. In tearing away from man the object of his production, therefore, estranged labor tears from him his *species-life*, his real objectivity as a member of the species and transforms his advantage over animals into the disadvantage that his inorganic body, nature, is taken from him.

Similarly, in degrading spontaneous, free activity to a means, estranged labor makes man's species-life a means to his physical existence.

The consciousness which man has of his species is thus transformed by estrangement in such a way that species[-life] becomes for him a means.

Estranged labor turns thus:

(3) *Man's species-being,* both nature and his spiritual species-property, into a being *alien* to him, into a *means* of his *individual existence.* It estranges from man his own body, as well as external nature and his spiritual aspect, his *human* aspect.

(4) An immediate consequence of the fact that man is estranged from the product of his labor, from his life activity, from his species-being, is the *estrangement of man* from *man.* When man confronts himself, he confronts the *other* man. What applies to a man's relation to his work, to the product of his labor and to himself, also holds of a man's relation to the other man, and to the other man's labor and object of labor.

In fact, the proposition that man's species-nature is estranged from him means that one man is estranged from the other, as each of them is from man's essential nature.

The estrangement of man, and in fact every relationship in which man [stands] to himself, is realized and expressed only in the relationship in which a man stands to other men.

Hence within the relationship of estranged labor each man views the other in accordance with the standard and the relationship in which he finds himself as a worker.

We took our departure from a fact of political economy—the estrangement of the worker and his production. We have formulated this fact in conceptual terms as *estranged, alienated* labor. We have analyzed this concept—hence analyzing merely a fact of political economy.

Let us now see, further, how the concept of estranged, alienated labor must express and present itself in real life.

If the product of labor is alien to me, if it confronts me as an alien power, to whom, then, does it belong?

To a being *other* than myself.

Who is this being?

The *gods*? To be sure, in the earliest times the principal production (for example, the building of temples, etc., in Egypt, India and Mexico) appears to be in the service of the gods, and the product belongs to the gods. However, the gods on their own were never the lords of labor. No more was *nature*. And what a contradiction it would be if, the more man subjugated nature by his labor and the more the miracles of the gods were rendered superfluous by the miracles of industry, the more man were to renounce the joy of production and the enjoyment of the product to please these powers.

The *alien* being, to whom labor and the product of labor belongs, in whose service labor is done and for whose benefit the product of labor is provided, can only be *man* himself.

If the product of labor does not belong to the worker, if it confronts him as an alien power, then this can only be because it belongs to some *other man than the worker*. If the worker's activity is a torment to him, to another it must give *satisfaction* and pleasure. Not the gods, not nature, but only man himself can be this alien power over man.

We must bear in mind the previous proposition that man's relation to himself becomes for him *objective* and *actual* through his relation to the other man. Thus, if the product of his labor, his labor objectified, is for him an *alien, hostile*, powerful object independent of him, then his position towards it is such that someone else is master of this object, someone who is alien, hostile, powerful, and independent of him. If he treats his own activity as an unfree activity, then he treats it as an activity performed in the service, under the dominion, the coercion, and the yoke of another man.

Every self-estrangement of man, from himself and from nature, appears in the relation in which he places himself and nature to men other than and differentiated from himself. For this reason religious self-estrangement necessarily appears in the relationship of the layman to the priest, or again to a mediator, etc., since we are here dealing with the intellectual world. In the real practical world self-estrangement can only become manifest through the real practical relationship to other men. The medium through which estrangement takes place is itself *practical*. Thus through estranged labor man not only creates his relationship to the object and to the act of production as to powers [in the manuscript *Menschen* (men) instead of *Mächte* (powers).—Ed.] that are alien and hostile to him; he also creates the relationship in which other men stand to his production and to his product, and the relationship in which he stands to these other men. Just as he creates his own production as the loss of his reality, as his punishment; his own product as a loss, as a product not belonging to him; so he creates the domination of the person who does not produce over production and over the product. Just as he estranges his own activity from himself, so he confers upon the stranger an activity which is not his own.

We have until now considered this relationship only from the standpoint of the worker and later on we shall be considering it also from the standpoint of the non-worker.

Through *estranged, alienated labor,* then, the worker produces the relationship to this labor of a man alien to labor and standing outside it. The relationship of the worker to labor creates the relation to it of the capitalist (or whatever one chooses to call the master of labor). *Private property* is thus the product, the result, the necessary consequence, of *alienated labor,* of the external relation of the worker to nature and to himself.

Private property thus results by analysis from the concept of *alienated labor,* i.e., of *alienated man,* of estranged labor, of estranged life, of *estranged* man.

True, it is as a result of the *movement of private property* that we have obtained the concept of *alienated labor (of alienated life)* in political economy. But on analysis of this concept it becomes clear that though private property appears to be the reason, the cause of alienated labor, it is rather its consequence, just as the gods are *originally* not the cause but the effect of man's intellectual confusion. Later this relationship becomes reciprocal.

Only at the culmination of the development of private property does this, its secret, appear again, namely, that on the one hand it is the *product* of alienated labor, and that on the other it is the *means* by which labor alienates itself, *the realization of this alienation.*

This exposition immediately sheds light on various hitherto unsolved conflicts.

(1) Political economy starts from labor as the real soul of production; yet to labor it gives nothing, and to private property everything. Confronting this contradiction, Proudhon has decided in favor of labor against private property.[25] We understand, however, that this apparent contradiction is the contradiction of *estranged labor* with itself, and that political economy has merely formulated the laws of estranged labor.

We also understand, therefore, that *wages* and *private property* are identical. Indeed, where the product, as the object of labor, pays for labor itself, there the wage is but a necessary consequence of labor's estrangement. Likewise, in the wage of labor, labor does not appear as an end in itself but as the servant of the wage. We shall develop this point later, and meanwhile will only draw some conclusions.[26]

An enforced *increase of wages* (disregarding all other difficulties, including the fact that it would only be by force, too, that such an increase, being an anomaly, could be maintained) would therefore be nothing but better *payment for the slave,* and would not win either for the worker or for labor their human status and dignity.

Indeed, even the *equality of wages,* as demanded by Proudhon, only transforms the relationship of the present-day worker to his labor into the relationship of all men to labor. Society would then be conceived as an abstract capitalist.

Wages are a direct consequence of estranged labor, and estranged labor is the direct cause of private property. The downfall of the one must therefore involve the downfall of the other.

(2) From the relationship of estranged labor to private property it follows further that the emancipation of society from private property, etc., from servitude, is expressed in the *political* form of the *emancipation of the workers*; not that *their* emancipation alone is at stake, but because the emancipation of the workers contains universal human emancipation—and it contains this because the whole of human servitude is involved in

---

[25] Apparently Marx refers to Proudhon's book *Qu'est-ce que la propri'eté?*, Paris, 1841.

[26] This passage shows that Marx here uses the category of wages in a broad sense, as an expression of antagonistic relations between the classes of capitalists and of wage-workers. Under "the wages" he understands "the wage-labour," the capitalist system as such. This idea was apparently elaborated in detail in that part of the manuscript which is now extant.

the relation of the worker to production, and all relations of servitude are but modifications and consequences of this relation.

Just as we have derived the concept of *private property* from the concept of *estranged, alienated labor* by *analysis*, so we can develop every *category* of political economy with the help of these two factors; and we shall find again in each category, e.g., trade, competition, capital, money only a *particular* and *developed* expression of these first elements.

But before considering this phenomenon, however, let us try to solve two other problems.

(1) To define the general *nature of private property*, as it has arisen as a result of estranged labor, in its relation to *truly human* and *social property*.

(2) We have accepted the *estrangement of labor*, its *alienation*, as a fact, and we have analyzed this fact. How, we now ask, does *man* come to *alienate*, to estrange, his *labor*? How is this estrangement rooted in the nature of human development? We have already gone a long way to the solution of this problem by *transforming* the question of the *origin of private property* into the question of the relation of *alienated labor* to the course of humanity's development. For when one speaks of *private property,* one thinks of dealing with something external to man. When one speaks of labor, one is directly dealing with man himself. This new formulation of the question already contains its solution.

As to (1): *The general nature of private property and its relation to truly human property.*

Alienated labor has resolved itself for us into two components which depend on one another, or which are but different expressions of one and the same relationship. *Appropriation* appears as *estrangement,* as *alienation*; and *alienation* appears as *appropriation, estrangement* as truly *becoming a citizen.*[27]

We have considered the one side—*alienated* labor in relation to the *worker* himself, i.e., the *relation of alienated labor to itself.* The product, the necessary outcome of this relationship, as we have seen, is the *property relation of the non-worker to the worker and to labor. Private property,* as the material, summary expression of alienated labor, embraces both relations—the *relation of the worker to work and to the product of his labor and to the non-worker,* and the relation of the *non-worker to the worker and to the product of his labor.*

Having seen that in relation to the worker who *appropriates* nature by means of his labor, this appropriation appears as estrangement, his own spontaneous activity as activity for another and as activity of another, vitality as a sacrifice of life, production of the object as loss of the object to an alien power, to an *alien* person—we shall now consider the relation to the worker, to labor and its object of this person who is *alien* to labor and the worker.

First it has to be noted that everything which appears in the worker as an *activity of alienation, of estrangement,* appears in the non-worker as a *state of alienation, of estrangement.*

Secondly, that the worker's *real, practical attitude* in production and to the product (as a state of mind) appears in the non-worker who confronting him as a *theoretical* attitude.

---

[27] This apparently refers to the conversion of individuals into members of civil society which is considered as the sphere of property, of material relations that determine all other relations. In this case Marx refers to the material relations of society based on private property and the antagonism of different classes.

Thirdly, the non-worker does everything against the worker which the worker does against himself; but he does not do against himself what he does against the worker.

Let us look more closely at these three relations.[28]

[ANTITHESIS OF CAPITAL AND LABOUR. LANDED PROPERTY AND CAPITAL]

... forms the interest on his capital. The worker is the subjective manifestation of the fact that capital is man wholly lost to himself, just as capital is the objective manifestation of the fact that labour is man lost to himself. But the *worker* has the misfortune to be a *living* capital, and therefore an *indigent* capital, one which loses its interest, and hence its livelihood, every moment it is not working. The *value* of the worker as capital rises according to demand and supply, and *physically* too his *existence*, his *life*, was and is looked upon as a supply of a *commodity* like any other. The worker produces capital, capital produces him—hence he produces himself, and man as *worker*, as a *commodity*, is the product of this entire cycle. To the man who is nothing more than a *worker*—and to him as a worker—his human qualities only exist insofar as they exist for capital *alien* to him. Because man and capital are alien, foreign to each other, however, and thus stand in an indifferent, external and accidental relationship to each other, it is inevitable that this foreignness should also appear as something *real*. As soon, therefore, as it occurs to capital (whether from necessity or caprice) no longer to be for the worker, he himself is no longer for himself: he has no work, hence no wages, and since he has no *existence as a human being* but only *as a worker*, he can go and bury himself, starve to death, etc. The worker exists as a worker only when he exists *for himself* as capital; and he exists as capital only when some *capital* exists *for him*. The existence of capital is *his* existence, his *life*; as it determines the tenor of his life in a manner indifferent to him.

Political economy, therefore, does not recognise the unemployed worker, the workingman, insofar as he happens to be outside this labour relationship. The rascal, swindler, beggar, the unemployed, the starving, wretched and criminal workingman—these are *figures* who do not exist for *political economy* but only for other eyes, those of the doctor, the judge, the grave-digger, and bum-bailiff, etc.; such figures are spectres outside its domain. For it, therefore, the worker's needs are but the one *need*—to maintain *him whilst he is working* and insofar as may be necessary to prevent the *race of labourers* from [dying] out. The wages of labour have thus exactly the same significance as the *maintenance* and *servicing* of any other productive instrument, or as the *consumption of capital* in general, required for its reproduction with interest, like the oil which is applied to wheels to keep them turning. Wages, therefore, belong to capital's and the capitalist's necessary *costs*, and must not exceed the bounds of this necessity. It was therefore quite logical for the English factory owners, before the Amendment Bill of 1834 to deduct from the wages of the worker the public charity which he was receiving out of the Poor Rate and to consider this to be an integral part of wages.[29]

Production does not simply produce man as a *commodity*, the *human commodity*, man in the role of *commodity*; it produces him in keeping with this role as a *mentally* and physically dehumanised being.—Immorality, deformity, and dulling of the workers and the capitalists.—Its product is *the self-conscious and self-acting commodity* ... the *human*

---

[28] At this point the first manuscript breaks off unfinished.—Ed.

[29] The Poor Law Amendment Act of 1834 deprived poor people considered able to work (including children) of any public relief except a place in the workhouse, where they were compelled to work.

commodity.... Great advance of Ricardo, Mill, etc., on Smith and Say, to declare the *existence* of the human being—the greater or lesser human productivity of the commodity—to be *indifferent* and even *harmful*. Not how many workers are maintained by a given capital, but rather how much interest it brings in, the sum-total of the annual *savings*, is said to be the true purpose of production.

It was likewise a great and consistent advance of modern English political economy, that, whilst elevating *labour* to the position of its *sole* principle, it should at the same time expound with complete clarity the *inverse* relation between wages and interest on capital, and the fact that the capitalist could normally *only* gain by pressing down wages, and vice versa. Not the defrauding of the consumer, but the capitalist and the worker taking advantage of each other, is shown to be the *normal* relationship.

The relations of private property contain latent within them the relation of private property as *labour*, the relation of private property as *capital*, and the *mutual relation* of these two to one another. There is the production of human activity as *labour*—that is, as an activity quite alien to itself, to man and to nature, and therefore to consciousness and the expression of life—the *abstract* existence of man as a mere *workman* who may therefore daily fall from his filled void into the absolute void—into his social, and therefore actual, non-existence. On the other hand, there is the production of the object of human activity as *capital*—in which all the natural and social characteristic of the object is *extinguished*; in which private property has lost its natural and social quality (and therefore every political and social illusion, and is not associated with any *apparently* human relations); in which the *selfsame* capital remains the *same* in the most diverse natural and social manifestations, totally indifferent to its *real* content. This contradiction, driven to the limit, is of necessity the limit, the culmination, and the downfall of the whole private-property relationship.

It is therefore another great achievement of modern English political economy to have declared rent of land to be the difference in the interest yielded by the worst and the best land under cultivation; to have exposed the landowner's romantic illusions—his alleged social importance and the identity of his interest with the interest of society, a view still maintained by *Adam Smith* after the Physiocrats; and to [have] anticipated and prepared the movement of the real world which will transform the landowner into an ordinary, prosaic capitalist, and thus simplify and sharpen the contradiction [between capital and labour] and. hasten its resolution. *Land* as *land*, and *rent* as *rent*, have lost their *distinction of rank* and become insignificant *capital* and *interest*—or rather, *capital* and *interest* that signify only money.

The *distinction* between capital and land, between profit and rent, and between both and wages, and *industry*, and *agriculture*, and *immovable* and *movable* private property—this distinction is not rooted in the nature of things, but is a *historical* distinction, a *fixed* historical moment in the formation and development of the contradiction between capital and labour. In industry, etc., as opposed to immovable landed property, is only expressed the way in which [industry] came into being and the contradiction to agriculture in which industry developed. This distinction only continues to exist as a *special* sort of work—as an *essential*, *important* and *life-embracing* distinction—so long as industry (town life) develops *over* and *against* landed property (aristocratic feudal life) and itself continues to bear the feudal character of its opposite in the form of monopoly, craft, guild, corporation, etc., within which labour still has a *seemingly social* significance, still the significance of the *real* community, and has not yet reached the stage of *indifference* to its content, of complete being-for-self,[30] i.e., of abstraction from all other being, and hence has not yet become *liberated* capital.

But liberated *industry*, industry constituted for itself as such, and *liberated capital*, are the necessary *development* of labour. The power of industry over its opposite is at once revealed in the emergence of *agriculture* as a real industry, while previously it left most of the work to the soil and to the slave of the soil, through whom the land cultivated itself. With the transformation of the slave into a *free* worker—i.e., into a *hireling*—the landlord himself is transformed into a captain of industry, into a capitalist—a transformation which takes place at first through the intermediacy of the *tenant farmer*. *The tenant farmer*, however, is the landowner's representative—the landowner's revealed *secret:* it is only through him that the landowner has his *economic* existence—his existence as a private proprietor—for the rent of his land only exists due to the competition between the farmers.

Thus, in the person of the *tenant farmer* the landlord *has* already become in essence a *common* capitalist. And this must come to pass, too, in actual fact: the capitalist engaged in agriculture—the tenant—must become a landlord, or vice versa. The tenant's *industrial hucksterism* is the *landowner's* industrial hucksterism, for the being of the former postulates the being of the latter.

But mindful of their contrasting origin, of their line of descent, the landowner knows the capitalist as his insolent, liberated, enriched slave of yesterday and sees himself as a *capitalist* who is threatened by him. The capitalist knows the landowner as the idle, cruel, egotistical master of yesterday; he knows that he injures him as a capitalist, but that it is to industry that he owes all his present social significance, his possessions and his pleasures; he sees in him a contradiction to *free* industry and to *free* capital—to capital independent of every natural limitation. This contradiction is extremely bitter, and each side tells the truth about the other. One need only read the attacks of immovable on movable property and vice versa to obtain a clear picture of their respective worthlessness. The landowner lays stress on the noble lineage of his property, on feudal souvenirs or reminiscences, the poetry of recollection, on his romantic disposition, on his political importance, etc.; and when he talks economics, it is *only* agriculture that he holds to be productive. At the same time he depicts his adversary as a sly, hawking, carping, deceitful, greedy, mercenary, rebellious, heartless and spiritless person who is estranged from the community and freely trades it away, who breeds, nourishes and cherishes competition, and with it pauperism, crime, and the dissolution of all social bonds, an extorting, pimping, servile, smooth, flattering, fleecing, dried-up rogue without honour, principles, poetry, substance, or anything else. (Amongst others see the Physiocrat *Bergasse*, whom Camille Desmoulins flays in his journal, *Révolutions de France et de Brabant;*[31] see von Vincke, Lancizolle, Haller, Leo, Kosegarten[32] and also *Sismondi.*)

Movable property, for its part, points to the miracles of industry and progress. It is

---

[30] In the manuscript "sein für sich selbst," which is an expression of Hegel's term "für sich' (for itself) as opposed to "an sich" (in itself). In the Hegelian philosophy the former means roughly explicit, conscious or defined in contrast to "an sich," a synonym for immature, implicit or unconscious.

[31] This refers to *Revolutions de France et de Brabant, par Camille Desmoulins. Second Trimestre, contenant mars, avril et mai, Paris, l'an lier,* 1790, N. 16, p. 139 sq.; N. 23, p. 425 sqq.; N. 26, p. 580 sqq.

[32] See on the other hand the garrulous, old-Hegelian theologian Funke who tells, after Herr Leo, with tears in his eyes how a slave had refused, when serfdom was abolished, to cease being the *property of the gentry.*[32] See also the patriotic visions *of Justus Möser,* which distinguish themselves by the fact that they never for a moment ... abandon the respectable, petty-bourgeois *"home-baked",* ordinary, narrow horizon of the philistine, and which nevertheless remain pure fancy. This contradiction has given them such an appeal to the German heart.—*Note* by Marx.

the child of modern times, whose legitimate, native-born son it is. It pities its adversary as a simpleton, *unenlightened* about his own nature (and in this it is completely right), who wants to replace moral capital and free labour by brute, immoral violence and serfdom. It depicts him as a Don Quixote, who under the guise of *bluntness, respectability,* the *general interest,* and *stability,* conceals incapacity for progress, greedy self-indulgence, selfishness, sectional interest, and evil intent. It declares him an artful *monopolist*; it pours cold water on his reminiscences, his poetry, and his romanticism by a historical and sarcastic enumeration of the baseness, cruelty, degradation, prostitution, infamy, anarchy and rebellion, of which romantic castles were the workshops.

It claims to have obtained political freedom for everybody; to have loosed the chains which fettered civil society; to have linked together different worlds; to have created trade promoting friendship between the peoples; to have created pure morality and a pleasant culture; to have given the people civilised needs in place of their crude wants, and the means of satisfying them. Meanwhile, it claims, the landowner—this idle, parasitic grain-profiteer—raises the price of the people's basic necessities and so forces the capitalist to raise wages without being able to increase productivity, thus impeding the growth of the nation's annual income, the accumulation of capital, and therefore the possibility of providing work for the people and wealth for the country, eventually cancelling it, thus producing a general decline—whilst he parasitically exploits every advantage of modern civilisation without doing the least thing for it, and without even abating in the slightest his feudal prejudices. Finally, let him—for whom the cultivation of the land and the land itself exist only as a source of money, which comes to him as a present—let him just take a look at his tenant farmer and say whether he himself is not a *downright, fantastic, sly* scoundrel who in his heart and in actual fact has for a long time belonged to *free* industry and to *lovely* trade, however much he may protest and prattle about historical memories and ethical or political goals. Everything which he can really advance to justify himself is true only of the *cultivator of the land* (the capitalist and the labourers), of whom the *landowner* is rather the *enemy.* Thus he gives evidence against himself. Movable property claims that *without* capital landed property is dead, worthless matter; that its civilised victory has discovered and made human labour the source of wealth in place of the dead thing. (See Paul Louis Courier, Saint-Simon, Ganilh, Ricardo, Mill, McCulloch and Destutt de Tracy and Michel Chevalier.)

The *real* course of development (to be inserted at this point) results in the necessary victory of the *capitalist* over the *landowner*—that is to say, of developed over undeveloped, immature private property—just as in general, movement must triumph over immobility; open, self-conscious baseness over hidden, unconscious baseness; *cupidity* over *self-indulgence*; the avowedly restless, adroit self-interest of *enlightenment* over the parochial, worldly-wise, respectable, idle and fantastic *self-interest of superstition*; and *money* over the other forms of private property.

Those states which sense something of the danger attaching to fully developed free industry, to fully developed pure morality and to fully developed philanthropic trade, try, but in vain, to hold in check the capitalisation of landed property.

Landed property in its distinction from capital is private property—capital—still afflicted with *local* and political prejudices; it is capital which has not yet extricated itself from its entanglement with the world and found the form proper to itself—capital *not* yet *fully developed.* It must achieve its abstract, that is, its *pure,* expression in the course of its *cosmogony.*

The character of *private property* is expressed by labour, capital, and the relations between these two. The movement through which these constituents have to pass is:

First. Unmediated or *mediated unity of the two.*

Capital and labour are at first still united. Then, though separated and estranged, they reciprocally develop and promote each other as *positive* conditions.

[*Second.*] *The two in opposition,* mutually excluding each other. The worker knows the capitalist as his own non-existence, and vice versa: each tries to rob the other of his existence.

[*Third.*] *Opposition* of each *to* itself. Capital = stored-up labour = labour. As such it splits into *capital itself* and its *interest,* and this latter again into *interest and profit.* The capitalist is completely sacrificed. He falls into the working class, whilst the worker (but only exceptionally) becomes a capitalist. Labour as a moment of capital—its costs. Thus the wages of labour—a sacrifice of capital.

Splitting of labour into *labour itself* and the *wages of labour.* The worker himself a capital, a commodity.

Clash of mutual contradictions.[33]

[PRIVATE PROPERTY AND LABOUR. POLITICAL ECONOMY AS A PRODUCT OF THE MOVEMENT OF PRIVATE PROPERTY]

Re. p. XXXVI The *subjective essence* of private property—*private property* as activity for itself,[34] as *subject,* as *person*—is *labour.* It is therefore evident that only the political economy which acknowledged *labour* as its principle—*Adam Smith*—and which therefore no longer looked upon private property as a mere *condition* external to man— that it is this political economy which has to be regarded on the one hand as a product of the real *energy* and the real *movement* of private property (it is a movement of private property become independent for itself in consciousness—the modern industry as Self)— as a product of modern *industry*—and on the other hand, as a force which has quickened and glorified the energy and development of modern industry and made it a power in the realm of *consciousness.* To this enlightened political economy, which has discovered— within private property—the *subjective essence* of wealth, the adherents of the monetary and mercantile system, who look upon private property *only as an objective* substance confronting men, seem therefore to be *fetishists, Catholics. Engels* was therefore right to call *Adam Smith* the *Luther of Political Economy.*[35] Just as Luther recognised *religion— faith*—as the substance of the external *world* and in consequence stood opposed to Catholic paganism—just as he superseded *external* religiosity by making religiosity the *inner* substance of man—just as he negated the priests outside the layman because he transplanted the priest into laymen's hearts, just so with wealth: wealth as something outside man and independent of him, and therefore as something to be maintained and asserted only in an external fashion, is done away with; that is, this *external, mindless objectivity* of wealth is done away with, with private property being incorporated in man himself and with man himself being recognised as its essence. But as a result man is brought within the orbit of private property, just as with Luther he is brought within the orbit of religion. Under the semblance of recognizing man, the political economy whose principle is labour rather carries to its logical conclusion the denial of man, since man

---

[33] Here ends the second manuscript.—Ed.

[34] The manuscript has "als für sich seiende Tätigkeit." For the meaning of the terms "für sich" and "an sich" in Hegel's philosophy see Note 25.

[35] See *Outlines of a Critique of Political Economy*

himself no longer stands in an external relation of tension to the external substance of private property, but has himself become this tense essence of private property. What was previously *being external to oneself*—man's actual externalization—has merely become the act of externalizing—the process of alienating. This political economy begins by seeming to acknowledge man (his independence, spontaneity, etc.); then, locating private property in man's own being, it can no longer be conditioned by the local, national or other *characteristics of private property* as of *something existing outside itself*. This political economy, consequently, displays a *cosmopolitan*, universal energy which overthrows every restriction and bond so as to establish itself instead as the *sole* politics, the sole universality, the sole limit and sole bond. Hence it must throw aside this *hypocrisy* in the course of its further development and come *out in its complete cynicism*. And this it does—untroubled by all the apparent contradictions in which it becomes involved as a result of this theory—by developing the idea of *labour* much *more one-sidedly*, and therefore *more sharply* and *more consistently*, as the sole *essence of wealth;* by proving the implications of this theory to be *anti-human* in character, in contrast to the other, original approach. Finally, by dealing the death-blow to *rent*—that last, *individual, natural* mode of private property and source of wealth existing independently of the movement of labour, that expression of feudal property, an expression which has already become wholly economic in character and therefore incapable of resisting political economy. (The *Ricardo* school.) There is not merely a relative growth in the *cynicism* of political economy from Smith through Say to Ricardo, Mill, etc., inasmuch as the implications of *industry* appear more developed and more contradictory in the eyes of the last-named; these later economists also advance in a positive sense constantly and consciously further than their predecessors in their estrangement from man. They do so, however, *only* because their science develops more consistently and truthfully. Because they make private property in its active form the subject, thus simultaneously turning man into the essence—and at the same time turning man as non-essentiality into the essence— the contradiction of reality corresponds completely to the contradictory being which they accept as their principle. Far from refuting it, the ruptured *world of industry* confirms their *self-ruptured* principle. Their principle is, after all, the principle of this rupture.

The physiocratic doctrine of *Dr. Quesnay* forms the transition from the mercantile system to Adam Smith. *Physiocracy* represents directly the decomposition of feudal property in *economic* terms, but it therefore just as directly represents its *economic metamorphosis* and restoration, save that now its language is no longer feudal but economic. All wealth is resolved into *land* and *cultivation* (agriculture). Land is not yet *capital*: it is still a *special* mode of its existence, the validity of which is supposed to lie in, and to *derive from*, its natural peculiarity. Yet land is a general natural *element*, whilst the mercantile system admits the existence of wealth only in the form of *precious metal*. Thus the *object* of wealth—its matter—has straightway obtained the highest degree of universality within the *bounds of nature*, insofar as even as *nature*, it is immediate objective wealth. And land only exists for *man* through labour, through agriculture.

Thus the subjective essence of wealth has already been transferred to labour. But at the same time agriculture is the *only productive* labour. Hence, labour is not yet grasped in its generality and abstraction: it is still bound to a particular *natural element as its matter*, and it is therefore only recognised in a *particular mode of existence determined by nature*. It is therefore still only a *specific, particular* alienation of man, just as its product is likewise conceived nearly [as] a specific form of wealth—due more to nature than to labour itself. The land is here still recognised as a phenomenon of nature independent of man—not yet as capital, i.e., as an aspect of labour itself. Labour appears, rather, as an aspect of the *land*. But since the fetishism of the old external wealth, of wealth existing only as an object, has been reduced to a very simple natural element, and since its essence—even if only partially and in a particular form—has been recognised within its subjective existence, the necessary step forward has been made in revealing the *general nature* of wealth and hence in the raising up of *labour* in its total absoluteness (i.e., its abstraction) as the *principle*. It is argued against physiocracy that *agriculture*, from the economic point of view—that is to say, from the only valid point of view—does not differ from any other industry; and that the *essence* of wealth, therefore, is not a *specific* form of labour bound to a particular element—a particular expression of labour—but *labour in general*.

Physiocracy denies *particular*, external, merely objective wealth by declaring labour to be the *essence* of wealth. But for physiocracy labour is at first only the *subjective essence* of landed property. (It takes its departure from the type of property which historically appears as the dominant and acknowledged type.) It turns only landed property into *alienated man*. It annuls its feudal character by declaring *industry* (agriculture) as its *essence*. But it disavows the world of industry and acknowledges the feudal system by declaring *agriculture* to be the *only* industry.

It is clear that if the *subjective essence* of industry is now grasped (of industry in opposition to landed property, i.e., of industry constituting itself as industry), this essence includes within itself its opposite. For just as industry incorporates annulled landed property, the *subjective* essence of industry at the same time incorporates the subjective essence of *landed property*.

Just as landed property is the first form of private property, with industry at first confronting it historically merely as a special kind of property—or, rather, as landed property's liberated slave—so this process repeats itself in the scientific analysis of the *subjective* essence of private property, *labour*. Labour appears at first only as *agricultural labour*, but then asserts itself as *labour* in general.

All wealth has become *industrial* wealth, the *wealth* of *labour*, and *industry* is accomplished labour, just as the *factory system* is the perfected essence of *industry*, that is of labour, and just as *industrial capital* is the accomplished objective form of private property.

We can now see how it is only at this point that private property can complete its dominion over man and become, in its most general form, a world-historical power.

[PRIVATE PROPERTY AND COMMUNISM. VARIOUS STAGES
OF DEVELOPMENT OF COMMUNIST VIEWS. CRUDE,
EQUALITARIAN COMMUNISM AND COMMUNISM AS
SOCIALISM COINCIDING WITH HUMANENESS]

Re. p. XXXIX. The antithesis between *lack of property* and *property*, so long as it is not comprehended as the antithesis of *labour and capital*, still remains an indifferent antithesis, not grasped in its *active connection*, in its *internal* relation, not yet grasped as a *contradiction*. It can find expression in this *first* form even without the advanced development of private property (as in ancient Rome, Turkey, etc.). It does not yet *appear* as having been established by private property itself. But labour, the subjective essence of private property as exclusion of property, and capital, objective labour as exclusion of labour, constitute *private property* as its developed state of contradiction—

hence a dynamic relationship driving towards resolution.

Re the same page. The transcendence of self-estrangement follows the same course as self-estrangement. *Private property* is first considered only in its objective aspect—but nevertheless with labour as its essence. Its form of existence is therefore *capital,* which is to be annulled "as such" (Proudhon). Or a *particular form* of labour—labour levelled down, fragmented, and therefore unfree—is conceived as the source of private property's *perniciousness* and of its existence in estrangement from men. For instance, *Fourier,* who, like the Physiocrats, also conceives *agricultural labour* to be at least the *exemplary* type, whereas *Saint-Simon* declares in contrast that *industrial labour* as such is the essence, and accordingly aspires to the *exclusive* rule of the industrialists and the improvement of the workers' condition. Finally, *communism* is the *positive* expression of annulled private property—at first as *universal* private property. By embracing this relation as a *whole,* communism is:

(1) In its first form only a *generalization* and *consummation* of it [of this relation]. As such it appears in a two-fold form: on the one hand, the dominion of *material* property bulks so large that it wants to destroy *everything* which is not capable of being possessed by all as *private property.* It wants to disregard talent, etc., in an *arbitrary* manner. For it the sole purpose of life and existence is direct, physical *possession.* The category of the *worker* is not done away with, but extended to all men. The relationship of private property persists as the relationship of the community to the world of things. Finally, this movement of opposing universal private property to private property finds expression in the brutish form of opposing to *marriage* (certainly a *form of exclusive private property*) the *community of women,* in which a woman becomes a piece of *communal* and *common* property. It may be said that this idea of the *community of women gives away the secret* of this as yet completely crude and thoughtless communism.[36] Just as woman passes from marriage to general prostitution,[37] so the entire world of wealth (that is, of man's objective substance) passes from the relationship of exclusive marriage with the owner of private property to a state of universal prostitution with the community. This type of communism—since it negates the *personality* of man in every sphere—is but the logical expression of private property, which is this negation. General *envy* constituting itself as a power is the disguise in which *greed* re-establishes itself and satisfies itself, only in *another* way. The thought of every piece of private property as such is *at least* turned against *wealthier* private property in the form of envy and the urge to reduce things to a common level, so that this envy and urge even constitute the essence of competition. Crude communism is only the culmination of this envy and of this levelling-down proceeding from the *preconceived* minimum. It has a *definite, limited* standard. How little

---

[36] Marx refers to the rise of the primitive, crude equalitarian tendencies among the representatives of utopian communism at the early stages of its development. Among the medieval religious communistic communities, in particular, there was current a notion of the common possession of women as a feature of the future society depicted in the spirit of consumer communism ideals. In 1534-35 the German Anabaptists, who seized power in Münster, tried to introduce polygamy in accordance with this view. Tommaso Campanella, the author of *Civitas Solis* (early 17th century), rejected monogamy in his ideal society. The primitive communistic communities were also characterised by asceticism and a hostile attitude to science and works of art. Some of these primitive equalitarian features, the negative attitude to the arts in particular, were inherited by the communist trends of the first half of the 19th century, for example, by the members of the French secret societies of the 1830s and 1840s ("worker-egalitarians," "humanitarians," and so on) comprising the followers of Babeuf (for a characterisation of these see Engels, "Progress of Social Reform on the Continent" (Karl Marx and Frederick Engels, *Collected Works,* Volume 3, pp. 396-97)).

[37] Prostitution is only a *specific* expression of the *general* prostitution of the *labourer,* and since it is a relationship in which falls not the prostitute alone, but also the one who prostitutes—and the latter's abomination is still greater—the capitalist, etc., also comes under this head.

this annulment of private property is really an appropriation is in fact proved by the abstract negation of the entire world of culture and civilisation, the regression to the *unnatural* simplicity of the *poor* and crude man who has few needs and who has not only failed to go beyond private property, but has not yet even reached it.

The community is only a community of *labour,* and equality of *wages* paid out by communal capital—by the *community* as the universal capitalist. Both sides of the relationship are raised to an *imagined* universality—*labour* as the category in which every person is placed, and *capital* as the acknowledged universality and power of the community.

In the approach to *woman* as the *spoil* and hand-maid of communal lust is expressed the infinite degradation in which man exists for himself, for the secret of this approach has its *unambiguous*, decisive, *plain* and undisguised expression in the relation of *man* to *woman* and in the manner in which the *direct* and *natural* species-relationship is conceived. The direct, natural, and necessary relation of person to person is the *relation of man* to *woman.* In this *natural* species-relationship man's relation to nature is immediately his relation to man, just as his relation to man is immediately his relation to nature—his own *natural* destination. In this relationship, therefore, is *sensuously manifested,* reduced to an observable *fact,* the extent to which the human essence has become nature to man, or to which nature to him has become the human essence of man. From this relationship one can therefore judge man's whole level of development. From the character of this relationship follows how much *man* as a *species-being,* as *man,* has come to be himself and to comprehend himself; the relation of man to woman is the *most natural* relation of human being to human being. It therefore reveals the extent to which man's *natural* behaviour has become *human,* or the extent to which the human essence in him has become a *natural* essence—the extent to which his *human nature* has come to be *natural* to him. This relationship also reveals the extent to which man's *need* has become a *human* need; the extent to which, therefore, the *other* person as a person has become for him a need—the extent to which he in his individual existence is at the same time a social being. The first positive annulment of private property—*crude* communism—is thus merely a *manifestation* of the vileness of private property, which wants to set itself up as the *positive community system.*

(2) Communism (α) still political in nature—democratic or despotic; (β) with the abolition of the state, yet still incomplete, and being still affected by private property, i.e., by the estrangement of man. In both forms communism already is aware of being reintegration or return of man to himself, the transcendence of human self-estrangement; but since it has not yet grasped the positive essence of private property, and just as little the *human* nature of need, it remains captive to it and infected by it. It has, indeed, grasped its concept, but not its essence.

(3) *Communism* as the *positive* transcendence of *private property* as *human self-estrangement,* and therefore as the real *appropriation* of the *human* essence by and for man; communism therefore as the complete return of man to himself as a *social* (i.e., human) being—a return accomplished consciously and embracing the entire wealth of previous development. This communism, as fully developed naturalism, equals humanism, and as fully developed humanism equals naturalism; it is the *genuine* resolution of the conflict between man and nature and between man and man—the true resolution of the strife between existence and essence, between objectification and self-confirmation, between freedom and necessity, between the individual and the species. Communism is the riddle of history solved, and it knows itself to be this solution.

The entire movement of history, just as its [communism's] *actual* act of genesis—the birth act of its empirical existence—is, therefore, for its thinking consciousness the *comprehended* and *known* process of its *becoming*. Whereas the still immature communism seeks an *historical* proof for itself—a proof in the realm of what already exists—among disconnected historical phenomena opposed to private property, tearing single phases from the historical process and focusing attention on them as proofs of its historical pedigree (a hobby-horse ridden hard especially by Cabet, Villegardelle, etc.). By so doing it simply makes clear that by far the greater part of this process contradicts its own claim, and that, if it has ever existed, precisely its being in the *past* refutes its pretension to *reality*.

It is easy to see that the entire revolutionary movement necessarily finds both its empirical and its theoretical basis in the movement of *private property*—more precisely, in that of the economy.

This *material*, immediately *perceptible* private property is the material perceptible expression of *estranged human* life. Its movement—production and consumption—is the *perceptible* revelation of the movement of all production until now, i.e., the realization or the reality of man. Religion, family, state, law, morality, science, art, etc., are only *particular* modes of production, and fall under its general law. The positive transcendence of *private property* as the appropriation of *human* life, is therefore the positive transcendence of all estrangement—that is to say, the return of man from religion, family, state, etc., to his *human*, i.e., *social,* existence. Religious estrangement as such occurs only in the realm of *consciousness,* of man's inner life, but economic estrangement is that of *real life;* its transcendence therefore embraces both aspects. It is evident that the *initial* stage of the movement amongst the various peoples depends on whether the true *recognised* life of the people manifests itself more in consciousness or in the external world—is more ideal or real. Communism begins from the outset (*Owen*) with atheism; but atheism is at first far from being *communism*; indeed, that atheism is still mostly an abstraction.

The philanthropy of atheism is therefore at first only *philosophical,* abstract philanthropy, and that of communism is at once *real* and directly bent on *action.*

We have seen how on the assumption of positively annulled private property man produces man—himself and the other man; how the object, being the direct manifestation of his individuality, is simultaneously his own existence for the other man, the existence of the other man, and that existence for him. Likewise, however, both the material of labour and man as the subject, are the point of departure as well as the result of the movement (and precisely in this fact, that they must constitute the *point of departure,* lies the historical *necessity* of private property). Thus the *social* character is the general character of the whole movement: *just as* society itself produces *man as man,* so is society *produced* by him. Activity and enjoyment, both in their content and in their *mode of existence*, are *social*: social activity and *social* enjoyment. The *human* aspect of nature exists only for *social* man; for only then does nature exist for him as a *bond* with man— as his existence for the other and the other's existence for him—and as the life-element of human reality. Only then does nature exist as the *foundation* of his own *human* existence. Only here has what is to him his *natural* existence become his *human* existence, and nature become man for him. Thus *society* is the complete unity of man with nature—the true resurrection of nature—the consistent naturalism of man and the consistent humanism of nature.

Social activity and social enjoyment exist by no means *only* in the form of some *directly* communal activity and directly *communal* enjoyment, although *communal* activity and *communal* enjoyment—i.e., activity and enjoyment which are manifested and affirmed in *actual direct association* with other men—will occur wherever such a *direct* expression of sociability stems from the true character of the activity's content and is appropriate to the nature of the enjoyment.

But also when I am active *scientifically*, etc.—an activity which I can seldom perform in direct community with others—then my activity is *social*, because I perform it as a *man*. Not only is the material of my activity given to me as a social product (as is even the language in which the thinker is active): my *own* existence *is* social activity, and therefore that which I make of myself, I make of myself for society and with the consciousness of myself as a social being.

My *general* consciousness is only the *theoretical* shape of that of which the *living* shape is the *real* community, the social fabric, although at the present day *general* consciousness is an abstraction from real life and as such confronts it with hostility. The *activity* of my general consciousness, as an activity, is therefore also my *theoretical* existence as a social being.

Above all we must avoid postulating "society" again as an abstraction vis-à-vis the individual. The individual *is the social being*. His manifestations of life—even if they may not appear in the direct form of *communal* manifestations of life carried out in association with others—are therefore an expression and confirmation of *social life*. Man's individual and species-life are not *different*, however much—and this is inevitable—the mode of existence of the individual is a more *particular* or more *general* mode of the life of the species, or the life of the species is a more *particular* or more *general* individual life.

In his *consciousness of species* man confirms his real *social life* and simply repeats his real existence in thought, just as conversely the being of the species confirms itself in species consciousness and exists for itself in its generality as a thinking being.

Man, much as he may therefore be a *particular* individual (and it is precisely his particularity which makes him an individual, and a real *individual* social being), is just as much the *totality*—the ideal totality—the subjective existence of imagined and experienced society for itself; just as he exists also in the real world both as awareness and real enjoyment of social existence, and as a totality of human manifestation of life.

Thinking and being are thus certainly *distinct*, but at the same time they are in unity with each other.

Death seems to be a harsh victory of the species over the *particular* individual and to contradict their unity. But the particular individual is only a *particular species-being*, and as such mortal.

(4) Just as *private property* is only the perceptible expression of the fact that man becomes *objective* for himself and at the same time becomes to himself a strange and inhuman object; just as it expresses the fact that the manifestation of his life is the alienation of his life, that his realisation is his loss of reality, is an *alien* reality: so, the positive transcendence of private property—i.e., the *perceptible* appropriation for and by man of the human essence and of human life, of objective man, of human *achievements* should not be conceived merely in the sense of *immediate*, one-sided *enjoyment*, merely in the sense of *possessing*, of *having*. Man appropriates his comprehensive essence in a comprehensive manner, that is to say, as a whole man. Each of his *human* relations to the world—seeing, hearing, smelling, tasting, feeling, thinking, observing, experiencing, wanting, acting, loving—in short, all the organs of his individual being, like those organs

which are directly social in their form, are in their *objective* orientation, or in their *orientation to the object,* the appropriation of the object, the appropriation of *human* reality. Their orientation to the object is the *manifestation of the human reality,*[38] it is human *activity* and human *suffering,* for suffering, humanly considered, is a kind of self-enjoyment of man.

Private property has made us so stupid and one-sided that an object is only *ours* when we have it—when it exists for us as capital, or when it is directly possessed, eaten, drunk, worn, inhabited, etc.,—in short, when it is *used* by us. Although private property itself again conceives all these direct realizations of possession only as *means of life,* and the life which they serve as means is the *life of private property*—labour and conversion into capital.

In the place of *all* physical and mental senses there has therefore come the sheer estrangement of *all* these senses, the sense of *having.* The human being had to be reduced to this absolute poverty in order that he might yield his inner wealth to the outer world. (On the category of "*having*", see *Hess* in the *Philosophy of the Deed*).

The abolition [*Aufhebung*] of private property is therefore the complete *emancipation* of all human senses and qualities, but it is this emancipation precisely because these senses and attributes have become, subjectively and objectively, *human.* The eye has become a *human* eye, just as its *object* has become a social, *human* object—an object made by man for man. The *senses* have therefore become directly in their practice *theoreticians.* They relate themselves to the thing for the sake of the thing, but the thing itself is an *objective human* relation to itself and to man,[39] and vice versa. Need or enjoyment have consequently lost its *egotistical* nature, and nature has lost its mere *utility* by use becoming *human* use.

In the same way, the senses and enjoyment of other men have become my *own* appropriation. Besides these direct organs, therefore, *social* organs develop in the *form* of society; thus, for instance, activity in direct association with others, etc., has become an organ for *expressing* my own *life,* and a mode of appropriating *human* life.

It is obvious that the *human* eye enjoys things in a way different from the crude, non-human eye; the human *ear* different from the crude ear, etc.

We have seen that man does not lose himself in his object only when the object becomes for him a *human* object or objective man. This is possible only when the object becomes for him a *social* object, he himself for himself a social being, just as society becomes a being for him in this object.

On the one hand, therefore, it is only when the objective world becomes everywhere for man in society the world of man's essential powers—human reality, and for that reason the reality of his *own* essential powers—that all *objects* become for him the *objectification* of himself, become objects which confirm and realise *his* individuality, become his objects: that is, *man himself* becomes the object. The *manner* in which they become *his* depends on the *nature of the objects* and on the nature of the *essential power* corresponding to *it*; for it is precisely the *determinate nature* of this relationship which shapes the particular, *real* mode of affirmation. To the *eye* an object comes to be other than it is to the *ear,* and the object of the eye *is* another object than the object of the *ear.* The specific character of each essential power is precisely its *specific essence,* and therefore also the specific mode of its objectification, of its *objectively actual,* living *being.* Thus man is affirmed in the objective world not only in the act of thinking, but

---

[38] For this reason it is just as highly varied as the *determinations* of human *essence* and *activities.*

[39] In practice I can relate myself to a thing humanly only if the thing relates itself humanly to the human being.

with *all* his senses.

On the other hand, let us look at this in its subjective aspect. Just as only music awakens in man the sense of music, and just as the most beautiful music has *no* sense for the unmusical ear—is [no] object for it, because my object can only be the confirmation of one of my essential powers—it can therefore only exist for me insofar as my essential power exists for itself as a subjective capacity; because the meaning of an object for me goes only so far as *my* sense goes (has only a meaning for a sense corresponding to that object)—for this reason the *senses* of the social man *differ* from those of the non-social man. Only through the objectively unfolded richness of man's essential being is the richness of subjective *human* sensibility (a musical ear, an eye for beauty of form—in short, *senses* capable of human gratification, senses affirming themselves as essential powers of *man*) either cultivated or brought into being. For not only the five senses but also the so-called mental senses, the practical senses (will, love, etc.), in a word, *human* sense, the human nature of the senses, comes to be by virtue of *its* object, by virtue of *humanised* nature. The *forming* of the five senses is a labour of the entire history of the world down to the present.

The *sense* caught up in crude practical need has only a *restricted* sense. For the starving man, it is not the human form of food that exists, but only its abstract existence as food. It could just as well be there in its crudest form, and it would be impossible to say wherein this feeding activity differs from that of *animals.* The care-burdened, poverty-stricken man has no *sense* for the finest play; the dealer in minerals sees only the commercial value but not the beauty and the specific character of the mineral: he has no mineralogical sense. Thus, the objectification of the human essence, both in its theoretical and practical aspects, is required to make man's *sense human,* as well as to create the *human sense* corresponding to the entire wealth of human and natural substance.

Just as through the movement of *private property*, of its wealth as well as its poverty—of its material and spiritual wealth and poverty—the budding society finds at hand all the material for this *development,* so *established* society produces man in this entire richness of his being produces the *rich* man *profoundly endowed with all the senses*—as its enduring reality.

We see how subjectivity and objectivity, spirituality and materiality, activity and suffering, lose their antithetical character, and—thus their existence as such antitheses only within the framework of society; we see how the resolution of the *theoretical* antitheses is *only* possible in a *practical* way, by virtue of the practical energy of man. Their resolution is therefore by no means merely a problem of understanding, but a *real* problem of life, which *philosophy* could not solve precisely because it conceived this problem as *merely* a theoretical one.

We see how the history of *industry* and the established *objective* existence of industry are the *open* book of *man's essential powers,* the perceptibly existing human *psychology.* Hitherto this was not conceived in its connection with man's *essential being,* but only in an external relation of utility, because, moving in the realm of estrangement, people could only think of man's general mode of being—religion or history in its abstract-general character as politics, art, literature, etc.—as the reality of man's essential powers and *man's species-activity.* We have before us the *objectified essential powers* of man in the form of *sensuous, alien, useful objects,* in the form of estrangement, displayed in *ordinary material industry* (which can be conceived either as a part of that general movement, or that movement can be conceived as a *particular* part of industry, since all human activity hitherto has been labour—that is, industry—activity estranged from itself).

A *psychology* for which this book, the part of history existing in the most perceptible and accessible form, remains a closed book, cannot become a genuine, comprehensive and *real* science. What indeed are we to think of a science which *airily* abstracts from this large part of human labour and which fails to feel its own incompleteness, while such a wealth of human endeavour, unfolded before it, means nothing more to it than, perhaps, what can be expressed in one word—"need", "*vulgar need*"?

The *natural sciences* have developed an enormous activity and have accumulated an ever-growing mass of material. Philosophy, however, has remained just as alien to them as they remain to philosophy. Their momentary unity was only a *chimerical illusion.* The will was there, but the power was lacking. Historiography itself pays regard to natural science only occasionally, as a factor of enlightenment, utility, and of some special great discoveries. But natural science has invaded and transformed human life all the more *practically* through the medium of industry; and has prepared human emancipation, although its immediate effect had to be the furthering of the dehumanization of man. *Industry* is the *actual*, historical relationship of nature, and therefore of natural science, to man. If, therefore, industry is conceived as the *exoteric* revelation of man's *essential powers,* we also gain an understanding of the human essence of nature or the natural essence of man. In consequence, natural science will lose its abstractly material—or rather, its idealistic—tendency, and will become the basis of *human* science, as it has already become—albeit in an estranged form—the basis of actual human life, and to assume *one* basis for life and a different basis for *science* is as a matter of course a lie. The nature which develops in human history—the genesis of human society—is man's *real* nature; hence nature as it develops through industry, even though in an *estranged* form, is true *anthropological* nature.

Sense-perception (see Feuerbach) must be the basis of all science. Only when it proceeds from sense-perception in the two-fold form of *sensuous* consciousness and *sensuous* need—is it *true* science. All history is the history of preparing and developing "man" to become the object of *sensuous* consciousness, and turning the requirements of "man as man" into his needs. History itself is a *real* part of *natural history*—of nature developing into man. Natural science will in time incorporate into itself the science of man, just as the science of man will incorporate into itself natural science: there will be *one* science.

Man is the immediate object of natural science; for immediate, *sensuous nature* for man is, immediately, human sensuousness (the expressions are identical)—presented immediately in the form of the *other* man sensuously present for him. Indeed, his own sense-perception first exists as human sensuousness for himself through the *other* man. But *nature* is the immediate object of the *science of man:* the first object of man—man—is nature, sensuousness; and the particular human sensuous essential powers can only find their self-understanding in the science of the natural world in general, just as they can find their objective realization only in *natural* objects. The element of thought itself—the element of thought's living expression—*language*—is of a sensuous nature. The *social* reality of nature, and *human* natural science, or the *natural science of man,* are identical terms.

It will be seen how in place of the *wealth and poverty* of political economy come the *rich human being* and the rich *human* need. The *rich* human being is simultaneously the human being *in need of* a totality of human manifestations of life—the man in whom his own realisation exists as an inner necessity, as *need.* Not only *wealth,* but likewise the *poverty* of man—under the assumption of socialism[40]—receives in equal measure a human and therefore social significance. Poverty is the passive bond which causes the human being to experience the need of the greatest wealth—the *other* human being. The dominion of the objective being in me, the sensuous outburst of my life activity, is *passion,* which thus becomes here the *activity* of my being.

(5) A *being* only considers himself independent when he stands on his own feet; and he only stands on his own feet when he owes his *existence* to himself. A man who lives by the grace of another regards himself as a dependent being. But I live completely by the grace of another if I owe him not only the maintenance of my life, but if he has, moreover, *created* my *life*—if he is the *source* of my life. When it is not of my own creation, my life has necessarily a source of this kind outside of it. The *Creation* is therefore an idea very difficult to dislodge from popular consciousness. The fact that nature and man exist on their own account is in*comprehensible* to it, because it contradicts everything *tangible* in practical life.

The creation of the *earth* has received a mighty blow from *geognosy*—i.e., from the science which presents the formation of the earth, the development of the earth, as a process, as a self-generation. *Generatio aequivoca*[41] is the only practical refutation of the theory of creation.[42]

Now it is certainly easy to say to the single individual what Aristotle has already said: You have been begotten by your father and your mother; therefore in you the mating of two human beings—a species-act of human beings—has produced the human being. You see, therefore, that even physically man owes his existence to man. Therefore you must not only keep sight of the *one* aspect—the *infinite* progression which leads you further to inquire: Who begot my father? Who his grandfather? etc. You must also hold on to the *circular movement* sensuously perceptible in that progress by which man repeats himself in procreation, *man* thus always remaining the subject. You will reply, however: I grant you this circular movement; now grant me the progress which drives me ever further until I ask: Who begot the first man, and nature as a whole? I can only answer you: Your question is itself a product of abstraction. Ask yourself how you arrived at that question. Ask yourself whether your question is not posed from a standpoint to which I cannot reply, because it is wrongly put. Ask yourself whether that progress as such exists for a reasonable mind. When you ask about the creation of nature and man, you are abstracting, in so doing, from man and nature. You postulate them as *non-existent,* and yet you want me to prove them to you as *existing.* Now I say to you: Give up your abstraction and you will also give up your question. Or if you want to hold on to your abstraction, then be consistent, and if you think of man and nature as *non-existent,* then think of yourself as non-existent, for you too are surely nature and man. Don't think, don't ask me, for as soon as you think and ask, your *abstraction* from the

---

[40] This part of the manuscript shows clearly the peculiarity of the terminology used by Marx in his works. At the time he had not worked out terms adequately expressing the conceptions of scientific communism he was then evolving and was still under the influence of Feuerbach in that respect. Hence the difference in the use of words in his early and subsequent, mature writings. In the *Economic and Philosophic Manuscripts of 1844* the word "socialism" is used to denote the stage of society at which it has carried out a revolutionary transformation, abolished private property, class antagonisms, alienation and so on. In the same sense Marx used the expression "communism equals humanism." At that time he understood the term "communism as such" not as the final goal of revolutionary transformation but as the process of this transformation, development leading up to that goal, a lower stage of the process.

[41] The spontaneous generation.—*Ed.*

[42] This expression apparently refers to the theory of the English geologist Sir Charles Lyell who, in his three-volume work *The Principles of Geology* (1830-33), proved the evolution of the earth's crust and refuted the popular theory of cataclysms. Lyell used the term "historical geology" for his theory. The term "geognosy" was introduced by the 18th-century German scientist Abraham Werner, a specialist in mineralogy, and it was used also by Alexander Humboldt.

existence of nature and man has no meaning. Or are you such an egotist that you conceive everything as nothing, and yet want yourself to exist?

You can reply: I do not want to postulate the nothingness of nature, etc. I ask you about its *genesis,* just as I ask the anatomist about the formation of bones, etc.

But since for the socialist man the *entire so-called history of the world* is nothing but the creation of man through human labour, nothing but the emergence of nature for man, so he has the visible, irrefutable proof of his *birth* through himself, of his *genesis.* Since the *real existence* of man and nature has become evident in practice, through sense experience, because man has thus become evident for man as the being of nature, and nature for man as the being of man, the question about an *alien* being, about a being above nature and man—a question which implies the admission of the unreality of nature and of man—has become impossible in practice. *Atheism,* as the denial of this unreality, has no longer any meaning, for atheism is a *negation of God,* and postulates *the existence of man* through this negation; but socialism as socialism no longer stands in any need of such a mediation. It proceeds from the *theoretically and practically sensuous consciousness* of man and of nature as the *essence.* Socialism is man's *positive self-consciousness,* no longer mediated through the abolition of religion, just as *real life* is man's positive reality, no longer mediated through the abolition of private property, through *communism.* Communism is the position as the negation of the negation, and is hence the *actual* phase necessary for the next stage of historical development in the process of human emancipation and rehabilitation. *Communism* is the necessary form and the dynamic principle of the immediate future, but communism as such is not the goal of human development, the form of human society.[43]

[THE MEANING OF HUMAN REQUIREMENTSS WHERE THERE IS PRIVATE PROPERTY AND UNDER SOCIALISM. THE DIFFERENCE BETWEEN EXTRAVAGANT WEALTH AND INDUSTRIAL WEALTH. DIVISION OF LABOUR IN BOURGEOIS SOCIETY]

[44] (7) We have seen what significance, given socialism, the *wealth* of human needs acquires, and what significance, therefore, both a *new mode of production* and a new *object* of production obtain: a new manifestation of the forces of human nature and a new enrichment of *human* nature. Under private property their significance is reversed: every person speculates on creating a *new* need in another, so as to drive him to fresh sacrifice, to place him in a new dependence and to seduce him into a new mode of *enjoyment* and therefore economic ruin. Each tries to establish over the other an alien power, so as thereby to find satisfaction of his own selfish need. The increase in the quantity of objects is therefore accompanied by an extension of the realm of the alien powers to which man is subjected, and every new product represents a new *potentiality* of mutual swindling and mutual plundering. Man becomes ever poorer as man, his need for money becomes

---

[43] This statement is interpreted differently by researchers. Many of them maintain that Marx here meant crude equalitarian communism, such as that propounded by Babeuf and his followers. While recognising the historic role of that communism, he thought it impossible to ignore its weak points. It seems more justifiable, however, to interpret this passage proceeding from the peculiarity of terms used in the manuscript (see Note 32). Marx here used the term "communism" to mean not the higher phase of classless society (which he at the time denoted as "socialism" or "communism equalling humanism") but movement (in various forms, including primitive forms of equalitarian communism at the early stage) directed at its achievement, a revolutionary transformation process of transition to it. Marx emphasised that this process should not be considered as an end in itself, but that it is a necessary, though a transitional, stage in attaining the future social system, which will be characterised by new features distinct from those proper to this stage.

[44] Page XI (in part) and pages XII and XIII are taken up by a text relating to the concluding chapter (see Note 28).

ever greater if he wants to master the hostile power. The power of his money declines in inverse proportion to the increase in the volume of production: that is, his neediness grows as the *power* of money increases.

The need for money is therefore the true need produced by the economic system, and it is the only need which the latter produces. The *quantity* of money becomes to an ever greater degree its sole *effective* quality. Just as it reduces everything to its abstract form, so it reduces itself in the course of its own movement to *quantitative* being. *Excess* and *intemperance* come to be its true norm. Subjectively, this appears partly in the fact that the extension of products and needs becomes a *contriving* and ever-calculating subservience to inhuman, sophisticated, unnatural and imaginary appetites. Private property does not know how to change crude need into human need. Its *idealism is fantasy, caprice* and *whim*; and no eunuch flatters his despot more basely or uses more despicable means to stimulate his dulled capacity for pleasure in order to sneak a favour for himself than does the industrial eunuch—the producer—in order to sneak for himself a few pieces of silver, in order to charm the golden birds, out of the pockets of his dearly beloved neighbours in Christ. He puts himself at the service of the other's most depraved fancies, plays the pimp between him and his need, excites in him morbid appetites, lies in wait for each of his weaknesses—all so that he can then demand the cash for this service of love. (Every product is a bait with which to seduce away the other's very being, his money; every real and possible need is a weakness which will lead the fly to the glue-pot. General exploitation of communal human nature, just as every imperfection in man, is a bond with heaven—an avenue giving the priest access to his heart; every need is an opportunity to approach one's neighbour under the guise of the utmost amiability and to say to him: Dear friend, I give you what you need, but you know the *conditio sine qua non*; you know the ink in which you have to sign yourself over to me; in providing for your pleasure, I fleece you.)

This estrangement manifests itself in part in that the sophistication of needs and of the means (of their satisfaction) on the one side produces a bestial barbarization, a complete, crude, abstract simplicity of need, on the other; or rather in that it merely reproduces itself in its opposite. Even the need for fresh air ceases to be a need for the worker. Man returns to a cave dwelling, which is now, however, contaminated with the pestilential breath of civilisation, and which he continues to occupy only *precariously,* it being for him an alien habitation which can be withdrawn from him any day—a place from which, if he does not pay, he can be thrown out any day. For this mortuary he has to *pay.* A dwelling in the light, which Prometheus in Aeschylus designated as one of the greatest boons, by means of which he made the savage into a human being, ceases to exist for the worker. Light, air, etc.—the simplest animal cleanliness—ceases to be a need for man. Filth, this stagnation and putrefaction of man—the *sewage* of civilisation (speaking quite literally)—comes to be the *element of life*—for him. Utter, unnatural depravation, putrefied nature, comes to be *his life-element.* None of his senses exist any longer, and (each has ceased to function) not only in its human fashion, but in an inhuman fashion, so that it does not exist even in an animal fashion. The crudest *methods (and instruments)* of human labour are coming back: the *treadmill* of the Roman slaves, for instance, is the means of production, the means of existence, of many English workers. It is not only that man has no human needs—even his animal needs cease to exist. The Irishman no longer knows any need now but the need to *eat,* and indeed only the need to eat *potatoes and scabby potatoes* at that, the worst kind of potatoes. But in each of their industrial towns England and France have already a little Ireland. The savage and the animal have at least the need to hunt, to roam, etc.—the need of companionship. The simplification of the machine, of labour is used to make a worker out of the human being still in the making, the completely immature human being, the child—whilst the worker has become a neglected child. The machine accommodates itself to the *weakness* of the human being in order to make the weak human being into a machine.

How the multiplication of needs and of the means (of their satisfaction) breeds the absence of needs and of means is demonstrated by the political economist (and by the capitalist: in general it is always empirical businessmen we are talking about when we refer to political economists, (who represent) their *scientific* creed and form of existence) as follows:

(1) By reducing the worker's need to the barest and most miserable level of physical subsistence, and by reducing his activity to the most abstract mechanical movement; thus he says: Man has no other need either of activity or of enjoyment. For he declares that this life, *too,* is *human* life and existence.

(2) By *counting the most meagre* form of life (existence) as the standard, indeed, as the general standard—general because it is applicable to the mass of men. He turns the worker into an insensible being lacking all needs, just as he changes his activity into a pure abstraction from all activity. To him, therefore, every *luxury* of the worker seems to be reprehensible, and everything that goes beyond the most abstract need—be it in the realm of passive enjoyment, or a manifestation of activity—seems to him a luxury. Political economy, this science of *wealth,* is therefore simultaneously the science of renunciation, of want, of *saving* and it actually reaches the point where it *spares* man the *need* of either fresh air or physical *exercise.* This science of marvellous industry is simultaneously the science of *asceticism,* and its true ideal is the *ascetic* but *extortionate* miser and the *ascetic* but *productive* slave. Its moral ideal is the worker who takes part of his wages to the savings-bank, and it has even found ready-made a servile art which embodies this pet idea: it has been presented, bathed in sentimentality, on the stage. Thus political economy—despite its worldly and voluptuous appearance—is a true moral science, the most moral of all the sciences. Self-renunciation, the renunciation of life and of all human needs, is its principal thesis. The less you eat, drink and buy books; the less you go to the theatre, the dance hall, the public house; the less you think, love, theorize, sing, paint, fence, etc., the more you *save*—the *greater* becomes your treasure which neither moths nor rust will devour—your capital. The less you are, the less you express your own life, the more you *have,* i.e., the greater is your *alienated* life, the greater is the store of your estranged being. Everything which the political economist takes from you in life and in humanity, he replaces for you in money and in *wealth;* and all the things which you cannot do, your money can do. It can eat and, drink, go to the dance hall and the theatre; it can travel, it can appropriate art, learning, the treasures of the past, political power—all this it can appropriate for you—it can buy all this: it is true *endowment.* Yet being all this, it *wants to* do nothing but create itself, buy itself; for everything else is after all its servant, and when I have the master I have the servant and do not need his servant. All passions and all activity must therefore be submerged in *avarice.* The worker may only have enough for him to want to live, and may only want to live in order to have that.

It is true that a controversy now arises in the field of political economy. The one side (Lauderdale, Malthus, etc.) recommends luxury and execrates thrift. The other (Say, Ricardo, etc.) recommends thrift and execrates luxury. But the former admits that it wants luxury in order to produce *labour* (i.e., absolute thrift); and the latter admits that it recommends thrift in order to produce *wealth* (i.e., luxury). The Lauderdale-Malthus school has the romantic notion that avarice alone ought not to determine the consumption of the rich, and it contradicts its own laws in advancing *extravagance* as a direct means of enrichment. Against it, therefore, the other side very earnestly and circumstantially proves that I do not increase but reduce my *possessions* by being extravagant. The Say-Ricardo school is hypocritical in not admitting that it is precisely whim and caprice which determine production. It forgets the "refined needs", it forgets that there would be no production without consumption; it forgets that as a result of competition production can only become more extensive and luxurious. It forgets that, according to its views, a thing's value is determined by use, and that use is determined by fashion. It wishes to see only "useful things" produced, but it forgets that production of too many useful things produces too large a *useless* population. Both sides forget that extravagance and thrift, luxury and privation, wealth and poverty are equal.

And you must not only stint the gratification of your immediate senses, as by stinting yourself on food, etc.: you must also spare yourself all sharing of general interests, all sympathy, all trust, etc., if you want to be economical, if you do not want to be ruined by illusions.

You must make everything that is yours *saleable,* i.e., useful. If I ask the political economist: Do I obey economic laws if I extract money by offering my body for sale, by surrendering it to another's lust? (The factory workers in France call the prostitution of their wives and daughters the nth working hour, which is literally correct.)—Or am I not acting in keeping with political economy if I sell my friend to the Moroccans? (And the direct sale of men in the form of a trade in conscripts, etc., takes place in all civilized countries.)—Then the political economist replies to me: You do not transgress my laws; but see what Cousin Ethics and Cousin Religion have to say about it. My *political economic* ethics and religion have nothing to reproach you with, but—But whom am I now to believe, political economy or ethics?—The ethics of political economy is *acquisition*, work, thrift, sobriety—but political economy promises to satisfy my needs.—The political economy of ethics is the opulence of a good conscience, of virtue, etc.; but how can I live virtuously if I do not live? And how can I have a good conscience if I do not know anything? It stems from the very nature of estrangement that each sphere applies to me a different and opposite yardstick—ethics one and political economy another; for each is a specific estrangement of man and focuses attention on a particular field of estranged essential activity, and each stands in an estranged relation to the other. Thus M. *Michel Chevalier* reproaches Ricardo with having ignored ethics. But Ricardo is allowing political economy to speak its own language, and if it does not speak ethically, this is not Ricardo's fault. M. Chevalier takes no account of political economy insofar as he moralizes, but he really and necessarily ignores ethics insofar as he practices political economy. The relationship of political economy to ethics, if it is other than an arbitrary, contingent and therefore unfounded and unscientific relationship, if it is not being posited for the sake of *appearance* but is meant to be *essential,* can only be the relationship of the laws of political economy to ethics. If there is no such connection, or if the contrary is rather the case, can Ricardo help it? Moreover, the opposition between political economy and ethics is only an *apparent* opposition and just as much no opposition *as it is* an opposition. All that happens is that political economy expresses moral laws in *its own way.*

Frugality as the principle of political economy is *most brilliantly* shown in its *theory of population.* There are too *many* people. Even the existence of men is a pure luxury; and if the worker is *"ethical"*, he will be *sparing* in procreation. (Mill suggests public acclaim for those who prove themselves continent in their sexual relations, and public rebuke for those who sin against such barrenness of marriage .... Is this not ethics, the teaching of asceticism?) The production of people appears as public destitution.

The meaning which production has in relation to the rich is seen *revealed* in the meaning which it has for the poor. Looking upwards the manifestation is always refined, veiled, ambiguous—outward appearance; downwards, it is rough, straightforward, frank—the real thing. The worker's *crude* need is a far greater source of gain than the *refined* need of the rich. The cellar dwellings in London bring more to those who let them than do the palaces; that is to say, with reference to the landlord they constitute *greater wealth,* and thus (to speak the language of political economy) greater *social* wealth.

Industry speculates on the refinement of needs, it speculates however just as much on their *crudeness,* but on their artificially produced crudeness, whose true enjoyment, therefore, is *self-stupefaction*—this *illusory* satisfaction of need this civilisation contained within the crude barbarism of need. The English gin shops are therefore the *symbolical* representations of private property. Their luxury reveals the true relation of industrial luxury and wealth to man. They are therefore rightly the only Sunday pleasures of the people which the English police treats at least mildly.

We have already seen how the political economist establishes the unity of labour and capital in a variety of ways: (1) Capital is *accumulated labour.* (2) The purpose of capital within production—partly, reproduction of capital with profit, partly, capital as raw material (material of labour), and partly, as an automatically *working instrument* (the machine is capital directly equated with labour)—is *productive labour.* (3) The worker is a capital. (4) Wages belong to costs of capital. (5) In relation to the worker, labour is the reproduction of his life-capital. (6) In relation to the capitalist, labour is an aspect of his capital's activity.

Finally, (7) the political economist postulates the original unity of capital and labour as the unity of the capitalist and the worker; this is the original state of paradise. The way in which these two aspects, as two persons, confront each other is for the political economist an *accidental* event, and hence only to be explained by reference to external factors. (See, Mill.)[45]

The nations which are still dazzled by the sensuous glitter of precious metals, and are therefore still fetish-worshippers of metal money, are not yet fully developed money-nations. Contrast of France and England. The extent to which the solution of theoretical riddles is the task of practice and effected through practice, the extent to which true practice is the condition of a real and positive theory, is shown, for example, in *fetishism.* The sensuous consciousness of the fetish-worshipper is different from that of the Greek, because his sensuous existence is different. The abstract enmity between sense and spirit is necessary so long as the human feeling for nature, the human sense of nature, and therefore also the *natural* sense of man, are not yet produced by man's own labour.

Equality is nothing but a translation of the German *"Ich = Ich"*[46] into the French, i.e., political form. Equality as the *basis* of communism is its political justification, and it is the same as when the German justifies it by conceiving man as *universal self-consciousness.* Naturally, the transcendence of the estrangement always proceeds from

[45] James Mill, *Elements of Political Economy.—Ed.*

[46] Apparently Marx refers to a formula of the German philosopher Fichte, an adherent of subjective idealism.

that form of the estrangement which is the dominant power: in Germany, *self-consciousness;* in France, *equality,* because it is politics; in England, real, material, *practical* need taking only itself as its standard. It is from this standpoint that Proudhon is to be criticized and appreciated.

If we characterize *communism* itself because of its character as negation of the negation, as the appropriation of the human essence through the intermediary of the negation of private property—as being not yet the true, self-originating position but rather a position originating from private property (...) in old-German fashion—in the way of Hegel's phenomenology—(...) finished as a *conquered moment* and (...) one might be satisfied by it, in his consciousness (...) of the human being only by real [...] transcendence of his thought now as before since with him therefore the real estrangement of the life of man remains, and remains all the more, the more one is conscious of it as such, hence it (the negation of this estrangement) can be accomplished solely by bringing about communism.

In order to abolish the *idea* of private property, the *idea* of communism is quite sufficient. It takes actual communist action to abolish actual private property. History will lead to it; and this movement, which *in theory* we already know to be a self-transcending movement, will constitute in actual fact a very rough and protracted process. But we must regard it as a real advance to have at the outset gained a consciousness of the limited character as well as of the goal of this historical movement—and a consciousness which reaches out beyond it.

When communist *artisans* associate with one another, theory, propaganda, etc., is their first end. But at the same time, as a result of this association, they acquire a new need—the need for society—and what appears as a means becomes an end. In this practical process the most splendid results are to be observed whenever French socialist workers are seen together. Such things as smoking, drinking, eating, etc., are no longer means of contact or means that bring them together. Association, society and conversation, which again has association as its end, are enough for them; the brotherhood of man is no mere phrase with them, but a fact of life, and the nobility of man shines upon us from their work-hardened bodies.

When political economy claims that demand and supply always balance each other, it immediately forgets that according to its own claim (theory of population) the supply of *people* always exceeds the demand, and that, therefore, in the essential result of the whole production process—the existence of man—the disparity between demand and supply gets its most striking expression.

The extent to which money, which appears as a means, constitutes true *power* and the sole *end*—the extent to which in general *the means* which turns me into a being, which gives me possession of the alien objective being, is an *end in itself* ... can be clearly seen from the fact that landed property, wherever land is the source of life, and *horse* and sword, wherever these are the *true means of life,* are also acknowledged as the true political powers in life. In the Middle Ages a social estate is emancipated as soon as it is allowed to carry the *sword.* Amongst nomadic peoples it is the *horse* which makes me a free man and a participant in the life of the community.

We have said above that man is regressing to the *cave dwelling,* etc.—but he is regressing to it in an estranged, malignant form. The savage in his cave—a natural element which freely offers itself for his use and protection—feels himself no more a stranger, or rather feels as much at home as a *fish* in water. But the cellar dwelling of the poor man is a hostile element, "a dwelling which remains an alien power and only gives itself up to him insofar as he gives up to it his own blood and sweat"—a dwelling which he cannot regard as his own hearth—where he might at last exclaim: "Here I am at home"—but where instead he finds himself *in someone else's* house, in the house of a *stranger* who always watches him and throws him out if he does not pay his rent. He is also aware of the contrast in quality between his dwelling and a human dwelling that stands in the *other* world, in the heaven of wealth.

Estrangement is manifested not only in the fact that *my* means of life belong to *someone else*, that which I desire is the inaccessible possession of *another,* but also in the fact that everything is itself something different from itself—that my activity is *something else* and that, finally (and this applies also to the capitalist), all is under (the sway) of in*human* power. There is a form of inactive, extravagant wealth given over wholly to pleasure, the enjoyer of which on the one hand *behaves* as a mere *ephemeral* individual frantically spending himself to no purpose, and also regards the slave-labour of others (human *sweat and blood*) as the prey of his cupidity. He therefore knows man himself, and hence also his own self, as a sacrificed and futile being. With such wealth contempt of man makes its appearance, partly as arrogance and as squandering of what can give sustenance to a hundred human lives, and partly as the infamous illusion that his own unbridled extravagance and ceaseless, unproductive consumption is the condition of the other's labour and therefore of his *subsistence.* He regards the realization of the *essential powers* of man only as the realization of his own excesses, his whims and capricious, bizarre notions. This wealth which, on the other hand, again knows wealth as a mere means, as something that is good for nothing but to be annihilated and which is therefore at once slave and master, at once magnanimous and base, capricious, presumptuous, conceited, refined, cultured and witty—this wealth has not yet experienced *wealth* as an utterly *alien power* over itself: it sees in it, rather, only its own power, and (not)a wealth but *enjoyment* (is its final) aim.

This [...] and the glittering illusion about the nature of wealth, blinded by sensuous appearances, is confronted by the *working, sober, prosaic, economical* industrialist who is quite enlightened about the nature of wealth, and who, while providing a wider sphere for the other's self—indulgence and paying fulsome flatteries to him in his products (for his products are just so many base compliments to the appetites of the spendthrift), knows how to appropriate for himself in the only *useful* way the other's waning power. If, therefore, industrial wealth appears at first to be the result of extravagant, fantastic wealth, yet its motion, the motion inherent in it, ousts the latter also in an active way. For the fall in the *rate of interest* is a necessary consequence and result of industrial development. The extravagant rentier's means therefore dwindle day by day in in*verse* proportion to the increasing possibilities and pitfalls of pleasure. Consequently, he must either consume his capital, thus ruining himself, or must become an industrial capitalist.... In the other hand, there is a direct, constant rise in the *rent of land* as a result of the course of industrial development; nevertheless, as we have already seen, there must come a time when landed property, like every other kind of property, is bound to fall within the category of profitably self-reproducing capital—and this in fact results from the same industrial development. Thus the squandering landowner, too, must either consume his capital, and thus be ruined, or himself become the farmer of his own estate—an agricultural industrialist.

The diminution in the interest on money, which Proudhon regards as the annulling of capital and as a tendency to socialize capital, is therefore in fact rather only a symptom of the total victory of working capital over squandering wealth—i.e., the transformation of all private property into industrial capital. It is a total victory of private property over all those of its qualities which are still in *appearance* human, and the complete subjection of the owner of private property to the essence of private property—labour. To be sure, the industrial capitalist also takes his pleasures. He does not by any means return to the unnatural simplicity of need; but his pleasure is only a side-issue—recreation— something subordinated to production; at the same time it is a *calculated* and, therefore, itself an *economical* pleasure. For he debits it to his capital's expense account, and what is squandered on his pleasure must therefore amount to no more than will be replaced with profit through the reproduction of capital. Pleasure is therefore subsumed under capital, and the pleasure-taking individual under the capital-accumulating individual, whilst formerly the contrary was the case. The decrease in the interest rate is therefore a symptom of the annulment of capital only inasmuch as it is a symptom of the growing domination of capital—of the estrangement which is growing and therefore hastening to its annulment. This is indeed the only way in which that which exists affirms its opposite.

The quarrel between the political economists about luxury and thrift is, therefore, only the quarrel between that political economy which has achieved clarity about the nature of wealth, and that political economy which is still afflicted with romantic, anti-industrial memories. Neither side, however, knows how to reduce the subject of the controversy to its simple terms, and neither therefore can make short work of the other.

Moreover, *rent of land qua* rent of land has been overthrown, since, contrary to the argument of the Physiocrats which maintains that the landowner is the only true producer, modern political economy has proved that the landowner as such is rather the only completely unproductive rentier. According to this theory, agriculture is the business of the capitalist, who invests his capital in it provided he can expect the usual profit. The claim of the Physiocrats—that landed property, as the sole productive property, should alone pay state taxes and therefore should alone approve them and participate in the affairs of state—is transformed into the opposite position that the tax on the rent of land is the only tax on unproductive income, and is therefore the only tax not detrimental to national production. It goes without saying that from this point of view also the political privilege of landowners no longer follows from their position as principal tax-payers.

Everything which Proudhon conceives as a movement of labour against capital is only the movement of labour in the determination of capital, of *industrial capital,* against capital not consumed as capital, i.e., not consumed industrially. And this movement is proceeding along its triumphant road—the road to the victory of *industrial* capital. It is clear, therefore, that only when *labour* is grasped as the essence of private property, can the economic process as such be analyzed in its real concreteness.

Society, as it appears to the political economist, is *civil society*[47] in which every individual is a totality of needs and only exists for the other person, as the other exists for him, insofar as each becomes a means for the other. The political economist reduces everything (just as does politics in its *Rights of Man*) to man, i.e., to the individual whom he strips of all determinateness so as to class him as capitalist or worker.

The *division of labour* is the economic expression of the *social character of labour* within the estrangement. Or, since *labour* is only an expression of human activity within

---

[47] In some of his early writings Marx already uses the term "*bürgerliche Gesellschaft*" to mean two things: (1) in a broader sense, the economic system of society regardless of the historical stage of its development, the sum total of material relations which determine political institutions and ideology, and (2) in the narrow sense, the material relations of bourgeois society (later on, that society as a whole), of capitalism. Hence, the term has been translated according to its concrete meaning in the context as "civil society" in the first case and "bourgeois society" in the second.

alienation, of the manifestation of life as the alienation of life, the *division of labour, too,* is therefore nothing else but the *estranged, alienated* positing of human activity as a *real activity of the species* or as *activity of man as a species-being.*

As for the *essence of the division of* labour—and of course the division of labour had to be conceived as a major driving force in the production of wealth as soon as *labour* was recognised as the *essence of private property*—i.e., as for the *estranged and alienated form of human activity as an activity of the species—the* political economists are very vague and self-contradictory about it.

Adam Smith: "This *division of labour* is not originally the effect of any human wisdom. It is the necessary, slow and gradual consequence of the propensity to truck, barter, and exchange one thing for another. This propensity" to trade is probably a - necessary consequence of the use of reason and of speech. It is common to all men, and to be found in no other race of animals." The animal, when it is grown up, is entirely independent. "Man has almost constant occasion for the help of others, and it is in vain for him to expect it from their benevolence only. He will be more likely to prevail if he can appeal to their personal interest, and show them that it-is for their own advantage to do for him what he requires of them. We address ourselves, not to their humanity but to their self-love, and never talk to them of our own necessities but of their advantages.

"As it is by treaty, by barter, and by purchase that we obtain from one another the greater part of those mutual good offices which we stand in need of, so it is this same trucking disposition which originally gives occasion to the division *of* labour. In a tribe of hunters or shepherds a particular person makes bows and arrows, for example, with more readiness and dexterity than any other. He frequently exchanges them for cattle or for venison with his companions; and he finds at last that he can in this manner get more cattle and venison than if he himself went to the field to catch them. From a regard to his own interest, therefore, the making of bows, etc., grows to be his chief business.

"The difference of natural talents in different men is not so much the cause as the effect of the division of labour.... Without the disposition to truck and exchange, every man must have procured to himself every necessary and conveniency of life. All must have had the same work to do, and there could have been no such difference of employment as could alone give occasion to any great difference of talents.

"As it is this disposition which forms that difference of talents among men so it is this same disposition which renders that difference useful. Many tribes of animals of the same species derive from nature a much more remarkable distinction of genius, than what, antecedent to custom and education, appears to take place among men. By nature a philosopher is not in talent and in intelligence half so different from a street porter, as a mastiff is from a greyhound, or a greyhound from a spaniel, or this last from a shepherd's dog. Those different tribes of animals, however, though all of the same species, are of scarce any use to one another. The mastiff cannot add to the advantages of his strength by making use of the swiftness of the greyhound, etc. The effects of these different talents or grades of intelligence, for want of the power or disposition to barter and exchange, cannot be brought into a common stock, and do not in the least contribute to the better accommodation and conveniency of the species. Each animal is still obliged to support and defend itself, separately and independently, and derives no sort of advantage from that variety of talents with which nature has distinguished its fellows. Among men, on the contrary, the most dissimilar geniuses are of use to one another; the different produces of their respective talents, by the general disposition to truck, barter, and exchange, being brought, as it were, into a common stock, where every man may purchase whatever part of the produce of other men's industry he has occasion for.

"As it is the power of exchanging that gives occasion to the division of labour, so the extent *of* this division must always be limited by the extent *of* that power, or, in other words, by the extent of the market. When the market is very small, no person can have any encouragement to dedicate himself entirely to one employment, for want of the power to exchange all that surplus part of the produce of his own labour, which is over and above his own consumption, for such parts of the produce of other men's labour as he has occasion for ..."

In an *advanced state* of society "every man thus lives by exchanging and becomes in some measure a merchant, and the society itself grows to be what is properly a commercial society."[48] (See Destutt de Tracy:[49] "Society is a series of reciprocal exchanges; commerce contains the whole essence of society.") ... The accumulation of capitals mounts with the division of labour, and vice versa."—So much for Adam Smith.

"If every family produced all that it consumed, society could keep going although no exchange of any sort took place; without being fundamental, exchange is indispensable in our advanced state of society. The division of labour is a skilful deployment of man's powers; it increases society's production-its power and its pleasures-but it curtails, reduces the ability of every person taken individually. Production cannot take place without exchange."—Thus J. B. Say.

"The powers inherent in man are his intelligence and his physical capacity for work. Those which arise from the condition of society consist of the capacity to *divide up labour* and to *distribute different jobs amongst different People* ... and the *power* to exchange *mutual services* and the products which constitute these means. The motive which impels a man to give his services to another is self -interest- he requires a reward for the services rendered. The right of exclusive private property is indispensable to the establishment of exchange amongst men." "Exchange and division of labour reciprocally condition each other." Thus *Skarbek*.

Mill presents developed exchange—*trade—as a consequence of the division of labour.*

"The agency of man can be traced to very simple elements. He can, in fact, do nothing more than produce motion. He can move things towards one another, and he can separate them from one another: the properties of matter perform all the rest." "In the employment of labour and machinery, it is often found that the effects can be increased by skilful distribution, by separating all those operations which have any tendency to impede one another, and by bringing together all those operations which can be made in any way to aid one another. As men in general cannot perform many different operations with the same quickness and dexterity with which they can by practice learn to perform a few, it is always an advantage to limit as much as possible the number of operations imposed upon each. For dividing labour, and distributing the powers of men and machinery, to the greatest advantage, it is in most cases necessary to operate upon a large scale; in other words, to produce the commodities in greater masses. It is this advantage which gives existence to the great manufactories; a few of which, placed in the most convenient situations, frequently supply not one country, but many countries, with as

---

[48] Adam Smith, Vol. I, p. 20.—*Ed.*

[49] *Élémens d'Idéologie, Traité de la Volonté et de ses Effets* (Elements of Ideology. Treatise on the Will and Its Effects), Paris, 1826, pp. 68, 78.—*Ed.*

much as they desire of the commodity produced."

Thus *Mill.*

The whole of modern political economy agrees, however, that division of labour and wealth of production, division of labour and accumulation of capital, mutually determine each other; just as it agrees that only private property which is *at liberty* to follow its own course can produce the most useful and comprehensive division of labour.

Adam Smith's argument can be summarised as follows: Division of labour bestows on labour infinite productive capacity. It stems from the *propensity to exchange and barter*, a specifically human propensity which is probably not accidental, but is conditioned by the use of reason and speech. The motive of those who engage in exchange is not *humanity* but *egoism*. The diversity of human talents is more the effect than the cause of the division of labour, i.e., of exchange. Besides, it is only the latter which makes such diversity useful. The particular attributes of the different breeds within a species of animal are by nature much more marked than the degrees of difference in human aptitude and activity. But because animals are unable to engage in *exchange*, no individual animal benefits from the difference in the attributes of animals of the same species but of different breeds. Animals are unable to combine the different attributes of their species, and are unable to contribute anything to the common advantage and comfort of the species. It is otherwise with men, amongst whom the most dissimilar talents and forms of activity are of use to one another, *because* they can bring their different products together into a common stock, from which each can purchase. As the division of labour springs from the propensity to *exchange,* so it grows and is limited by the *extent of exchange—by the extent of the market.* In advanced conditions, every man is a *merchant,* and society is a *commercial society. Say* regards *exchange* as accidental and not fundamental. Society could exist without it. It becomes indispensable in the advanced state of society. Yet *production* cannot take place *without it.* Division of labour is a *convenient, useful* means—a skilful deployment of human powers for social wealth; but it reduces the *ability of each person taken individually.* The last remark is a step forward on the part of Say.

Skarbek distinguishes the *individual powers inherent in* man—intelligence and the physical capacity for work—from the powers *derived from* society—exchange *and division of* labour, which mutually condition one another. But the necessary premise of exchange is *private property.* Skarbek here expresses in an objective form what Smith, Say, Ricardo, etc., say when they designate *egoism and self-interest as* the basis of exchange, and *buying and selling* as the *essential and adequate* form of exchange.

Mill presents *trade* as the consequence of the *division of labour.* With him human activity is reduced to *mechanical motion.* Division of labour and use of machinery promote wealth of production. Each person must be entrusted with as small a sphere of operations as possible. Division of labour and use of machinery, in their turn, imply large-scale production of wealth, and hence of products. This is the reason for large manufactories.

The examination of *division of labour* and *exchange* is of extreme interest, because these are *perceptibly alienated* expressions of human *activity and essential power* as a *species* activity and species power.

To assert that *division of labour and exchange* rest on *private property* is nothing but asserting that *labour* is the essence of private property—an assertion which the political economist cannot prove and which we wish to prove for him. Precisely in the fact that *division of labour and exchange* are aspects of private property lies the twofold proof, on the one hand that *human* life required *private property for* its realization, and on the other hand that it now requires the supersession of private property.

Division of labour and exchange are the *two phenomena* which lead the political economist to boast of the social character of his science, while in the same breath he gives unconscious expression to the contradiction in his science—the motivation of society by unsocial, particular interests.

The factors we have to consider are: Firstly, the *propensity to exchange*—the basis of which is found in egoism—is regarded as the cause or reciprocal effect of the division of labour. Say regards exchange as not *fundamental* to the nature of society. Wealth—production—is explained by division of labour and exchange. The impoverishment of individual activity, and its loss of character as a result of the division of labour, are admitted. Exchange and division of labour are acknowledged as the sources of the great *diversity of human talents*—a diversity which in its turn becomes *useful* as a result of exchange. Skarbek divides man's essential powers of production—or productive powers—into two parts: (1) those which are individual and inherent in him—his intelligence and his special disposition, or capacity, for work; and (2) those *derived* from society and not from the actual individual—division of labour and exchange.

Furthermore, the division of labour is limited by the market. Human labour is simple *mechanical* motion: the main work is done by the material properties of the objects. The fewest possible operations must be apportioned to any one individual. Splitting-up of labour and concentration of capital; the insignificance of individual production and the production of wealth in large quantities. Meaning of free private property within the division of labour.

[THE POWER OF MONEY IN BOURGEOIS SOCIETY]

If man's *feelings*, passions, etc., are not merely anthropological phenomena in the (narrower) sense, but truly *ontological*[50] affirmations of being (of nature), and if they are only really affirmed because their *object* exists for them as a *sensual* object, then it is clear that:

1. They have by no means merely one mode of affirmation, but rather that the distinct character of their existence, of their life, is constituted by the distinct mode of their affirmation. In what manner the object exists for them, is the characteristic mode of their *gratification.*

2. Wherever the sensuous affirmation is the direct annulment of the object in its independent form (as in eating, drinking, working up of the object, etc.), this is the affirmation of the object.

3. Insofar as man, and hence also his feeling, etc., is *human,* the affirmation of the object by another is likewise his own gratification.

4. Only through developed industry—i.e., through the medium of private property—does the ontological essence of human passion come into being, in its totality as well as in its humanity; the science of man is therefore itself a product of man's own practical activity.

5. The meaning of private property—apart from its estrangement—is the *existence of essential objects* for man, both as objects of enjoyment and as objects of activity.

By possessing the *property* of buying everything, by possessing the property of

---

[50] Ontology—in some philosophic systems a theory about being, about the nature of things.

appropriating all objects, *money* is thus the *object* of eminent possession. The universality of its *property* is the omnipotence of its being. It is therefore regarded as an omnipotent being. Money is the *procurer* between man's need and the object, between his life and his means of life. But *that which* mediates *my* life for me, also *mediates* the existence of other people for me. For me it is the *other* person.

> "What, man! confound it, hands and feet
> And head and backside, all are yours!
> And what we take while life is sweet,
> Is that to be declared not ours?
> > "Six stallions, say, I can afford,
> > Is not their strength my property?
> > I tear along, a sporting lord,
> > As if their legs belonged to me."
>
> Goethe: *Faust* (Mephistopheles)

Shakespeare in *Timon of Athens:*

> "Gold? Yellow, glittering, precious gold?
> No, Gods, I am no idle votarist! ...
> Thus much of this will make black white, foul fair,
> Wrong right, base noble, old young, coward valiant.
> ... Why, this
> Will lug your priests and servants from your sides,
> Pluck stout men's pillows from below their heads:
> This yellow slave
> Will knit and break religions, bless the accursed;
> Make the hoar leprosy adored, place thieves
> And give them title, knee and approbation
> With senators on the bench: This is it
> That makes the wappen'd widow wed again;
> She, whom the spital-house and ulcerous sores
> Would cast the gorge at, this embalms and spices
> To the April day again. Come, damned earth,
> Thou common whore of mankind, that put'st odds
> Among the rout of nations."[51]

And also later:

> "O thou sweet king-killer, and dear divorce
> 'Twixt natural son and sire! thou bright defiler
> Of Hymen's purest bed! thou valiant Mars!
> Thou ever young, fresh, loved and delicate wooer
> Whose blush doth thaw the consecrated snow
> That lies on Dian's lap! Thou *visible God!*
> That solder'st *close impossibilities,*

---

[51] Shakespeare, *Timon of Athens*, Act 4, Sc. 3. (Marx quotes the Schlegel-Tieck translation.)—*Ed.*

And makest them kiss! That speak'st with every tongue,
To every purpose! O thou touch of hearts!
Think, thy slave man rebels, and by thy virtue
Set them into confounding odds, that beasts
May have the world in empire!"[52]

Shakespeare excellently depicts the real nature of *money*. To understand him, let us begin, first of all, by expounding the passage from Goethe.

That which is for me through the medium of *money*—that for which I can pay (i.e., which money can buy)—that am *I myself,* the possessor of the money. The extent of the power of money is the extent of my power. Money's properties are my—the possessor's—properties and essential powers. Thus, what I *am* and *am capable of* is by no means determined by my individuality. I *am* ugly, but I can buy for myself the *most beautiful* of women. Therefore I am not *ugly,* for the effect of *ugliness*—its deterrent power—is nullified by money. I, according to my individual characteristics, am *lame,* but money furnishes me with twenty-four feet. Therefore I am not lame. I am bad, dishonest, unscrupulous, stupid; but money is honoured, and hence its possessor. Money is the supreme good, therefore its possessor is good. Money, besides, saves me the trouble of being dishonest: I am therefore presumed honest. I am *brainless,* but money is the *real brain* of all things and how then should its possessor be brainless? Besides, he can buy clever people for himself, and is he who has power over the clever not more clever than the clever? Do not I, who thanks to money am capable of *all* that the human heart longs for, possess all human capacities? Does not my money, therefore, transform all my incapacities into their contrary?

If *money* is the bond binding me to *human* life, binding society to me, connecting me with nature and man, is not money the bond of all *bonds?* Can it not dissolve and bind all ties? Is it not, therefore, also the universal *agent of separation?* It is the coin that really *separates* as well as the real *binding agent*—the [universal][53] *galvano-chemical* power of society.

Shakespeare stresses especially two properties of money:

1. It is the visible divinity—the transformation of all human and natural properties into their contraries, the universal confounding and distorting of things: impossibilities are soldered together by it.

2. It is the common whore, the common procurer of people and nations.

The distorting and confounding of all human and natural qualities, the fraternization of impossibilities—the *divine* power of money—lies in its *character* as men's estranged, alienating and self-disposing *species-nature.* Money is the alienated *ability of mankind.*

That which I am unable to do as a *man,* and of which therefore all my individual essential powers are incapable, I am able to do by means of *money.* Money thus turns each of these powers into something which in itself it is not—turns it, that is, into its *contrary.*

If I long for a particular dish or want to take the mail-coach because I am not strong enough to go by foot, money fetches me the dish and the mail-coach: that is, it converts my wishes from something in the realm of imagination, translates them from their meditated, imagined or desired existence into their *sensuous, actual* existence—from imagination to life, from imagined being into real being. In effecting this mediation,

---

[52] Ibid.
[53] An end of the page is torn out in the manuscript.—*Ed.*

[money] is the *truly creative* power.

No doubt the *demand* also exists for him who has no money, but his demand is a mere thing of the imagination without effect or existence for me, for a third party, for the [others], and which therefore remains even for me *unreal* and *objectless*. The difference between effective demand based on money and ineffective demand based on my need, my passion, my wish, etc., is the difference between *being* and *thinking*, between that which *exists* within me merely as an idea and the idea which exists as a *real object* outside of me.

If I have no money for travel, I have no need—that is, no real and realizable need—to travel. If I have the *vocation* for study but no money for it, I have no vocation for study—that is, no *effective*, no *true* vocation. On the other hand, if I have really *no* vocation for study but have the will and the money for it, I have an *effective* vocation for it. *Money* as the external, universal *medium* and *faculty* (not springing from man as man or from human society as society) for turning an *image into reality* and *reality into a mere image*, transforms the *real essential powers of man and nature* into what are merely abstract notions and therefore *imperfections* and tormenting chimeras, just as it transforms *real imperfections and chimeras*—essential powers which are really impotent, which exist only in the imagination of the individual—into *real powers and faculties*. In the light of this characteristic alone, money is thus the general distorting of *individualities* which turns them into their opposite and confers contradictory attributes upon their attributes.

Money, then, appears as this *distorting* power both against the individual and against the bonds of society, etc., which claim to be *entities* in themselves. It transforms fidelity into infidelity, love into hate, hate into love, virtue into vice, vice into virtue, servant into master, master into servant, idiocy into intelligence, and intelligence into idiocy.

Since money, as the existing and active concept of value, confounds and confuses all things, it is the general *confounding and confusing* of all things—the world upside-down—the confounding and confusing of all natural and human qualities.

He who can buy bravery is brave, though he be a coward. As money is not exchanged for any one specific quality, for any one specific thing, or for any particular human essential power, but for the entire objective world of man and nature, from the standpoint of its possessor it therefore serves to exchange every quality for every other, even contradictory, quality and object: it is the fraternization of impossibilities. It makes contradictions embrace.

Assume *man* to be *man* and his relationship to the world to be a human one: then you can exchange love only for love, trust for trust, etc. If you want to enjoy art, you must be an artistically cultivated person; if you want to exercise influence over other people, you must be a person with a stimulating and encouraging effect on other people. Every one of your relations to man and to nature must be a *specific expression*, corresponding to the object of your will, of your *real individual* life. If you love without evoking love in return—that is, if your loving as loving does not produce reciprocal love; if through a *living expression* of yourself as a loving person you do not make yourself a *beloved one*, then your love is impotent—a misfortune.

[CRITIQUE OF THE HEGELIAN DIALECTIC AND PHILOSOPHY AS A WHOLE]

(6) This is perhaps the place at which, by way of explanation and justification, we might offer some considerations in regard to the Hegelian dialectic generally and

especially its exposition in the *Phänomenologie* and *Logik* and also, lastly, the relation (to it) of the modern critical movement.[54]

So powerful was modern German criticism's preoccupation with the past—so completely was its development entangled with the subject-matter—that here prevailed a completely uncritical attitude to the method of criticising, together with a complete lack of awareness about the *apparently formal*, but really *vital* question: how do we now stand as regards the Hegelian *dialectic?* This lack of awareness about the relationship of modern criticism to the Hegelian philosophy as a whole and especially to the Hegelian dialectic has been so great that critics like *Strauss* and *Bruno Bauer* still remain within the confines of the Hegelian logic; the former completely so and the latter at least implicitly so in his *Synoptiker* (where, in opposition to Strauss, he replaces the substance of "abstract nature" by the "self-consciousness" of abstract man), and even in *Das entdeckte Christenthum*. Thus in *Das entdeckte Christenthum*, for example, you get:

"As though in positing the world, self-consciousness does not posit that which is different [from itself] and in what it is creating it does not create itself, since it in turn annuls the difference between what it has created and itself, since it itself has being only in creating and in the movement—as though its purpose were not this movement?" etc.; or again: "They" (the French materialists) "have not yet been able to see that it is only as the movement of self-consciousness that the movement of the universe has actually come to be for itself, and achieved unity with itself."

Such expressions do not even show any verbal divergence from the Hegelian approach, but on the contrary repeat it word for word.

How little consciousness there was in relation to the Hegelian dialectic during the act of criticism (Bauer, the *Synoptiker*), and how little this consciousness came into being even after the act of material criticism, is proved by Bauer when, in his *Die gute Sache der Freiheit,* he dismisses the brash question put by Herr Gruppe—"What about logic now?"—by referring him to future critics.[55]

But even now—now that *Feuerbach* both in his *Thesen* in the *Anekdota* and, in detail, in the *Philosophie der Zukunft* has in principle overthrown the old dialectic and philosophy; now that that school of criticism, on the other hand, which was incapable of accomplishing this, has all the same seen it accomplished and has proclaimed itself pure, resolute, absolute criticism that has come into the clear with itself; now that this criticism, in its spiritual pride, has reduced the whole process of history to the relation between the rest of the world and itself (the rest of the world, in contrast to itself, falling under the category of "the masses") and dissolved all dogmatic antitheses into the *single* dogmatic antithesis of its own cleverness and the stupidity of the world—the antithesis of the critical Christ and Mankind, the "*rabble*"; now that daily and hourly it has demonstrated

---

[54] Originally the section on the Hegelian dialectic was apparently conceived by Marx as a philosophical digression in the section of the third manuscript which is published under the heading "Private Property and Communism" and was written together with other sections as an addition to separate pages of the second manuscript (see pp. 93-108 of this book). Therefore Marx marked the beginning of this section (p. XI in the manuscript) as point 6, considering it to be the continuation of the five points of the preceding section. He marked as point 7 the beginning of the following section, headed "Human Requirements and Division of Labour Under the Rule of Private Property," on page XIV of the manuscript. However, when dealing with this subject on subsequent pages of his manuscript, Marx decided to collect the whole material into a separate, concluding chapter and mentioned this in his draft Preface. The chapter, like a number of other sections of the manuscript, was not finished. While writing it, Marx made special excerpts from the last chapter ("Absolute Knowledge") of Hegel's *Phänomenologie des Geistes*, which are in the same notebook as the third manuscript (these excerpts are not reproduced in this edition).

[55] The reference is not quite accurate. On page 193 of the work mentioned, Bruno Bauer polemises not against the anti-Hegelian Herr Gruppe but against the Right Hegelian Marheineke.

its own excellence against the dullness of the masses; now, finally, that it has proclaimed the critical *Last Judgment* in the shape of an announcement that the day is approaching when the whole of decadent humanity will assemble before it and be sorted by it into groups, each particular mob receiving its *testimonium paupertatis*; now that it has made known in print its superiority to human feelings as well as its superiority to the world, over which it sits enthroned in sublime solitude, only letting fall from time to time from its sarcastic lips the ringing laughter of the Olympian Gods—even now, after all these delightful antics of idealism (i.e., of Young Hegelianism) expiring in the guise of criticism—even now it has not expressed the suspicion that the time was ripe for a critical settling of accounts with the mother of Young Hegelianism—the Hegelian dialectic—and even had nothing to say about its critical attitude towards the Feuerbachian dialectic. This shows a completely uncritical attitude to itself.

Feuerbach is the only one who has a *serious, critical* attitude to the Hegelian dialectic and who has made genuine discoveries in this field. He is in fact the true conqueror of the old philosophy. The extent of his achievement, and the unpretentious simplicity with which he, Feuerbach, gives it to the world, stand in striking contrast to the opposite attitude [of the others].

Feuerbach's great achievement is:

(1) The proof that philosophy is nothing else but religion rendered into thought and expounded by thought, i.e., another form and manner of existence of the estrangement of the essence of man; hence equally to be condemned;

(2) The establishment of *true materialism* and of *real science,* by making the social relationship of "man to man" the basic principle of the theory;

(3) His opposing to the negation of the negation, which claims to be the absolute positive, the self-supporting positive, positively based on itself.

Feuerbach explains the Hegelian dialectic (and thereby justifies starting out from the positive facts which we know by the senses) as follows:

Hegel sets out from the estrangement of substance (in logic, from the infinite, abstractly universal)—from the absolute and fixed abstraction; which means, put popularly, that he sets out from religion and theology.

Secondly, he annuls the infinite, and posits the actual, sensuous, real, finite, particular (philosophy, annulment of religion and theology).

Thirdly, he again annuls the positive and restores the abstraction, the infinite—restoration of religion and theology.

Feuerbach thus conceives the negation of the negation *only* as a contradiction of philosophy with itself—as the philosophy which affirms theology (the transcendent, etc.) after having denied it, and which it therefore affirms in opposition to itself.

The positive position or self-affirmation and self-confirmation contained in the negation of the negation is taken to be a position which is not yet sure of itself, which is therefore burdened with its opposite, which is doubtful of itself and therefore in need of proof, and which, therefore, is not a position demonstrating itself by its existence—not an acknowledged position; hence it is directly and immediately confronted by the position of sense-certainty based on itself.[56]

But because Hegel has conceived the negation of the negation, from the point of view of the positive relation inherent in it, as the true and only positive, and from the point of view of the negative relation inherent in it as the only true act and spontaneous

---

[56] Feuerbach also defines the negation of the negation, the definite concept, as thinking surpassing itself in thinking and as thinking wanting to be directly awareness, nature, reality.

activity of all being, he has only found the *abstract, logical, speculative* expression for the movement of history, which is not yet the *real* history of man as a given subject, but only the *act of creation,* the *history of the origin* of man. We shall explain both the abstract form of this process and the difference between this process as it is in Hegel in contrast to modern criticism, in contrast to the same process in Feuerbach's *Wesen des Christenthums,* or rather the *critical* form of this in Hegel still uncritical process.

Let us take a look at the Hegelian system. One must begin with Hegel's *Phänomenologie,* the true point of origin and the secret of the Hegelian philosophy.

Phenomenology.

A. *Self-consciousness.*

I. *Consciousness.* (a) Certainty at the level of sense-experience; or the "this" and meaning. (b) *Perception,* or the thing with its properties, and *deception.* (g) Force and understanding, appearance and the supersensible world.

II. *Self-consciousness.* The truth of certainty of self. (a) Independence and dependence of self-consciousness; mastery and servitude. (b) Freedom of self-consciousness. Stoicism, scepticism, the unhappy consciousness.

III. *Reason.* Reason's certainty and reason's truth. (a) Observation as a process of reason. Observation of nature and of self-consciousness. (b) Realisation of rational self-consciousness through its own activity. Pleasure and necessity. The law of the heart and the insanity of self-conceit. Virtue and the course of the world. (c) The individuality which is real in and for itself. The spiritual animal kingdom and the deception or the real fact. Reason as lawgiver. Reason which tests laws.

B. *Mind.*

I. *True* mind, ethics. II. Mind in self-estrangement, culture. III. Mind certain of itself, morality.

C. Religion.

Natural religion; *religion of art; revealed* religion.

D. *Absolute knowledge.*

Hegel's *Encyklopädie,* beginning as it does with logic, with *pure speculative thought,* and ending with *absolute knowledge*—with the self-conscious, self-comprehending philosophic or absolute (i.e., superhuman) abstract mind—is in its entirety nothing but the *display,* the self-objectification, of the *essence* of the philosophic mind, and the philosophic mind is nothing but the estranged mind of the world thinking within its self-estrangement—i.e., comprehending itself abstractly. *Logic*—mind's *coin of the realm,* the speculative or *mental value* of man and nature—its essence which has grown totally indifferent to all real determinateness, and hence unreal—is *alienated thinking,* and therefore thinking which abstracts from nature and from real man: *abstract* thinking. Then: *The externality of this abstract thinking* ... *nature,* as it is for this abstract thinking. Nature is external to it—its self-loss; and it apprehends nature also in an external fashion, as abstract thought, but as alienated abstract thinking. Finally, *mind,* this thinking returning home to its own point of origin—the thinking which as the anthropological, phenomenological, psychological, ethical, artistic and religious mind is not valid for itself, until ultimately it finds itself, and affirms itself, as *absolute* knowledge and hence absolute, i.e., abstract, mind, thus receiving its conscious embodiment in the mode of existence corresponding to it. For its real mode of existence is *abstraction.*

There is a double error in Hegel.

The first emerges most clearly in the *Phänomenologie*, the birth-place of the Hegelian philosophy. When, for instance, wealth, state-power, etc., are understood by Hegel as entities estranged from the *human* being, this only happens in their form as thoughts ... They are thought-entities, and therefore merely an estrangement of *pure*, i.e., abstract, philosophical thinking. The whole process therefore ends with absolute knowledge. It is precisely abstract thought from which these objects are estranged and which they confront with their presumption of reality. The *philosopher*—who is himself an abstract form of estranged man—takes himself as the *criterion* of the estranged world. The whole *history of the alienation process* and the whole *process of the retraction* of the alienation is therefore nothing but the *history of the production* of abstract (i.e., absolute) thought—of logical, speculative thought. The *estrangement*, which therefore forms the real interest of the transcendence of this alienation, is the opposition of *in itself* and *for itself*, of *consciousness and self-consciousness*, of *object and subject*—that is to say, it is the opposition between abstract thinking and sensuous reality or real sensuousness within thought itself. All other oppositions and movements of these oppositions are but the *semblance*, the *cloak*, the *exoteric* shape of these oppositions which alone matter, and which constitute the *meaning* of these other, profane oppositions. It is not the fact that the human being *objectifies himself inhumanly*, in opposition to himself, but the fact that he *objectifies himself* in *distinction* from and in *opposition* to abstract thinking, that constitutes the posited essence of the estrangement and the thing to be superseded.

The appropriation of man's essential powers, which have become objects—indeed, alien objects—is thus in the *first place* only an *appropriation* occurring in *consciousness*, in *pure thought*, i.e., in *abstraction:* it is the appropriation of these objects as *thoughts* and as *movements of thought*. Consequently, despite its thoroughly negative and critical appearance and despite the genuine criticism contained in it, which often anticipates far later development, there is already latent in the *Phänomenologie* as a germ, a potentiality, a secret, the uncritical positivism and the equally uncritical idealism of Hegel's later works—that philosophic dissolution and restoration of the existing empirical world. *In the second place*: the vindication of the objective world for man—for example, the realization that *sensuous* consciousness is not an *abstractly* sensuous consciousness but a *humanly* sensuous consciousness, that religion, wealth, etc., are but the estranged world of *human* objectification, of *man's* essential powers put to work and that they are therefore but the *path* to the true *human* world—this appropriation or the insight into this process appears in Hegel therefore in this form, that *sense, religion,* state power, etc., are *spiritual* entities; for only *mind* is the *true* essence of man, and the true form of mind is thinking mind, theological, speculative mind. The *human character* of nature and of the nature created by history—man's products—appears in the form that they are *products* of abstract mind and as such, therefore, phases of *mind—thought-entities*. The *Phänomenologie* is, therefore, a hidden, mystifying and still uncertain criticism; but inasmuch as it depicts man's *estrangement*, even though man appears only as mind, there lie concealed in it *all* the elements of criticism, already *prepared* and *elaborated* in a manner often rising far above the Hegelian standpoint. The "unhappy consciousness", the "honest consciousness", the struggle of the "noble and base consciousness", etc., etc.— these separate sections contain, but still in an estranged form, the *critical* elements of whole spheres such as religion, the state, civil life, etc. Just as *entities, objects,* appear as thought-entities, so the *subject* is always *consciousness* or *self-consciousness;* or rather the object appears only as *abstract* consciousness, man only as *self-consciousness:* the distinct forms of estrangement which make their appearance are, therefore, only various forms of consciousness and self-consciousness. Just as *in itself* abstract consciousness (the form in which the object is conceived) is merely a moment of distinction of self-consciousness, what appears as the result of the movement is the identity of self-consciousness with consciousness—absolute knowledge—the movement of abstract thought no longer directed outwards but proceeding now only within its own self: that is to say, the dialectic of pure thought is the result.

The outstanding achievement of Hegel's *Phänomenologie* and of its final outcome, the dialectic of negativity as the moving and generating principle, is thus first that Hegel conceives the self-creation of man as a process, conceives objectification as loss of the object, as alienation and as transcendence of this alienation; that he thus grasps the essence of *labour* and comprehends objective man—true, because real man—as the outcome of man's *own labour*. The *real, active* orientation of man to himself as a species-being, or his manifestation as a real species-being (i.e., as a human being), is only possible if he really brings out all his *species-powers*—something which in turn is only possible through the cooperative action of all of mankind, only as the result of history—and treats these powers as objects: and this, to begin with, is again only possible in the form of estrangement.

We shall now demonstrate in detail Hegel's one-sidedness and limitations as they are displayed in the final chapter of the *Phänomenologie*, "Absolute Knowledge"—a chapter which contains the condensed spirit of the *Phänomenologie*, the relationship of the *Phänomenologie* to speculative dialectic, and also Hegel's *consciousness* concerning both and their relationship to one another.

Let us provisionally say just this much in advance: Hegel's standpoint is that of modern political economy. He grasps *labour* as the *essence* of man—as man's essence which stands the test: he sees only the positive, not the negative side of labour. Labour is *man's coming-to-be* for *himself* within *alienation*, or as *alienated* man. The only labour which Hegel knows and recognises is *abstractly mental* labour. Therefore, that which constitutes the *essence* of philosophy—the *alienation of man who knows himself*, or *alienated* science *thinking itself*—Hegel grasps as its essence; and in contradistinction to previous philosophy he is therefore able to combine its separate aspects, and to present his philosophy as *the* philosophy. What the other philosophers did—that they grasped separate phases of nature and of abstract self-consciousness, namely, of human life as phases of self-consciousness—is *known* to Hegel as the *doings* of philosophy. Hence his science is absolute.

Let us now turn to our subject.

"Absolute Knowledge". The last chapter of the "Phänomenologie".

The main point is that the *object of consciousness* is nothing else but *self-consciousness*, or that the object is only *objectified self-consciousness*—self-consciousness as object. (Positing of man = self-consciousness).

The issue, therefore, is to surmount the *object of consciousness*. *Objectivity* as such is regarded as an *estranged* human relationship which does not correspond to the *essence of man*, to self-consciousness. The *reappropriation* of the objective essence of man, produced within the orbit of estrangement as something alien, therefore denotes not only the annulment of *estrangement*, but of *objectivity* as well. Man, that is to say, is regarded as a *non-objective, spiritual* being.

The movement of *surmounting the object of consciousness* is now described by Hegel in the following way:

The *object* reveals itself not merely as *returning* into the *self*—this is according to

Hegel the *one-sided* way of apprehending this movement, the grasping of only one side. Man is equated with self. The self, however, is only the *abstractly* conceived man—man created by abstraction. Man *is* selfish. His eye, his ear, etc., are *selfish*. In him every one of his essential powers has the quality of *selfhood*. But it is quite false to say on that account "*self-consciousness* has eyes, ears, essential powers". *Self-consciousness* is rather a quality of human nature, of the human eye, etc.; it is not human nature that is a quality of *self-consciousness*.

The self-abstracted entity, fixed for itself, is man as *abstract egoist*—egoism raised in its pure abstraction to the level of thought. (We shall return to this point later.)

For Hegel the *human being—man*—equals *self-consciousness*. All estrangement of the human being is therefore *nothing* but *estrangement of self-consciousness*. The estrangement of self-consciousness is not regarded as an *expression*—reflected in the realm of knowledge and thought—of the *real* estrangement of the human being. Instead, the *actual* estrangement—that which appears real—is according to its *innermost*, hidden nature (which is only brought to light by philosophy) nothing but the *manifestation* of the estrangement of the real human essence, of *self-consciousness*. The science which comprehends this is therefore called *phenomenology*. All reappropriation of the estranged objective essence appears therefore, as incorporation into self-consciousness: The man who takes hold of his essential being is *merely* the self-consciousness which takes hold of objective essences. Return of the object into the self is therefore the reappropriation of the object.

Expressed in *all its aspects*, the *surmounting of the object of consciousness* means:

(1) That the object as such presents itself to consciousness as something vanishing. (2) That it is the alienation of self-consciousness which posits thinghood. (3) That this alienation has, not merely a *negative* but *a positive* significance. (4) That it has this meaning not merely *for us* or intrinsically, but *for self-consciousness itself*. (5) *For self-consciousness*, the negative of the object, or its annulling of itself, has *positive* significance—or it *knows* this futility of the object—because of the fact that it alienates itself, for in this alienation it posits *itself* as object, or, for the sake of the indivisible unity of *being-for-self*, posits the object as itself. (6) On the other hand, this contains likewise the other moment, that self-consciousness has also just as much superseded this alienation and objectivity and resumed them into itself, being thus *at home* in *its* other-being *as such*. (7) This is the movement of consciousness and this is therefore the totality of its moments. (8) Consciousness must similarly be related to the object in the totality of its determinations and have comprehended it in terms of each of them. This totality of its determinations makes the object *intrinsically a spiritual being;* and it becomes so in truth for consciousness through the apprehending of each one of the determinations as *self*, or through what was called above the *spiritual* attitude to them.

As to (1): That the object as such presents itself to consciousness as something vanishing—this is the above-mentioned *return of the object into the self*.

As to (2): The *alienation of self-consciousness* posits *thinghood*. Because man equals self-consciousness, his alienated, objective essence, or *thinghood*, equals *alienated self-consciousness*, and *thinghood* is thus posited through this alienation (thinghood being *that* which is an *object for man* and an object for him is really only that which is to him an essential object, therefore his *objective* essence. And since it is not *real man,* nor therefore *nature*—man being *human nature*—who as such is made the subject, but only the abstraction of man—self-consciousness—thinghood cannot be anything but alienated self-consciousness). It is only to be expected that a living, natural being equipped and endowed with objective (i.e., material) essential powers should have real natural objects of his essence; and that his self-alienation should lead to the positing of a *real*, objective world, but within the framework of *externality*, and, therefore, an overwhelming world not belonging to his own essential being. There is nothing incomprehensible or mysterious in this. It would be mysterious, rather, if it were otherwise. But it is equally clear that a *self-consciousness* by its alienation can posit only *thinghood*, i.e., only an abstract thing, a thing of abstraction and not a *real* thing. It is clear, further, that thinghood is therefore utterly without any *independence*, any *essentiality* vis-à-vis self-consciousness; that on the contrary it is a mere creature—something *posited* by self-consciousness. And what is posited, instead of confirming itself, is but confirmation of the act of positing which for a moment fixes its energy as the product, and gives it the *semblance*—but only for a moment—of an independent, real substance.

Whenever real, corporeal *man*, man with his feet firmly on the solid ground, man exhaling and inhaling all the forces of nature, *posits* his real, objective *essential powers* as alien objects by his externalisation, it is not the *act of positing* which is the subject in this process: it is the subjectivity of *objective* essential powers, whose action, therefore, must also be something objective. An objective being acts objectively, and he would not act objectively if the objective did not reside in the very nature of his being. He only creates or posits objects, because he is posited by objects—because at bottom he is *nature*. In the act of positing, therefore, this objective being does not fall from his state of "pure activity" into *a creating of the object*; on the contrary, his *objective* product only confirms his *objective* activity, his activity as the activity of an objective, natural being.

Here we see how consistent naturalism or humanism is distinct from both idealism and materialism, and constitutes at the same time the unifying truth of both. We see also how only naturalism is capable of comprehending the action of world history.

Man is directly a *natural being*. As a natural being and as a living natural being he is on the one hand endowed with *natural powers, vital powers*—he is an *active* natural being. These forces exist in him as tendencies and abilities—as *instincts*. On the other hand, as a natural, corporeal, sensuous objective being he is a *suffering*, conditioned and limited creature, like animals and plants. That is to say, the *objects* of his instincts exist outside him, as *objects* independent of him; yet these objects are *objects* that he *needs*—essential *objects*, indispensable to the manifestation and confirmation of his essential powers. To say that man is a *corporeal*, living, real, sensuous, objective being full of natural vigour is to say that he has *real, sensuous objects* as the object of his being or of his life, or that he can only *express* his life in real, sensuous objects. *To be* objective, natural and sensuous, and at the same time to have object, nature and sense outside oneself, or oneself to be object, nature and sense for a third party, is one and the same thing. *Hunger* is a natural *need;* it therefore needs a *nature* outside itself, an *object* outside itself, in order to satisfy itself, to be stilled. Hunger is an acknowledged need of my body for an *object* existing outside it, indispensable to its integration and to the expression of its essential being. The sun is the *object* of the plant—an indispensable object to it, confirming its life—just as the plant is an object of the sun, being an *expression* of the life-awakening power of the sun, of the sun's *objective es*sential power.

A being which does not have its nature outside itself is not a *natural* being, and plays no part in the system of nature. A being which has no object outside itself is not an objective being. A being which is not itself an object for some third being has no being for its *object;* i.e., it is not objectively related. Its being is not objective.

A unobjective being is a *non-being*.

Suppose a being which is neither an object itself, nor has an object. Such a being, in the first place, would be the *unique* being: there would exist no being outside it—it would exist solitary and alone. For as soon as there are objects outside me, as soon as I am not *alone,* I am *another—another reality* than the object outside me. For this third object I am thus a *different reality* than itself; that is, I am *its* object. Thus, to suppose a being which is not the object of another being is to presuppose that *no* objective being exists. As soon as I have an object, this object has me for an object. But a *non-objective* being is an unreal, non-sensuous thing—a product of mere thought (i.e., of mere imagination)—an abstraction. To be *sensuous,* that is, to be really existing, means to be an object of sense, to be a *sensuous* object, to have sensuous objects outside oneself—objects of one's sensuousness. To be sensuous is to *suffer.*

Man as an objective, sensuous being is therefore a *suffering* being—and because he feels that he suffers, a *passionate* being. Passion is the essential power of man energetically bent on its object.

But man is not merely a natural being: he is a *human* natural being. That is to say, he is a being for himself. Therefore he is a *species-being,* and has to confirm and manifest himself as such both in his being and in his knowing. Therefore, *human* objects are not natural objects as they immediately present themselves, and neither is *human sense* as it immediately *is*—as it is objectively—*human* sensibility, human objectivity. Neither nature objectively nor nature subjectively is directly given in a form adequate to the *human* being. And as everything natural has to *come into being, man* too has his act of origin—*history*—which, however, is for him a known history, and hence as an act of origin it is a conscious self-transcending act of origin. History is the true natural history of man (on which more later).

Thirdly, because this positing of thinghood is itself only an illusion, an act contradicting the nature of pure activity, it has to be cancelled again and thinghood denied.

Re 3, 4, 5 and 6. (3) This externalization of consciousness has not merely a *negative* but a *positive* significance, and (4) it has this meaning not merely *for us* or intrinsically, but for consciousness itself. *For consciousness* the negative of the object, its annulling of itself, has *positive* significance—i.e., consciousness *knows* this nullity of the object—because it alienates *itself;* for, in this alienation it *knows* itself as object, or, for the sake of the indivisible unity of *being-for-itself,* the object as itself. (6) On the other hand, there is also this other moment in the process, that consciousness has also just as much superseded this alienation and objectivity and resumed them into itself, being thus *at home* in its *other-being as such.*

As we have already seen, the appropriation of what is estranged and objective, or the annulling of objectivity in the form of *estrangement* (which has to advance from indifferent strangeness to real, antagonistic estrangement), means likewise or even primarily for Hegel that it is *objectivity* which is to be annulled, because it is not the *determinate* character of the object, but rather its *objective* character that is offensive and constitutes estrangement for self-consciousness. The object is therefore something negative, self-annulling—a *nullity.* This nullity of the object has not only a negative but a *positive* meaning for consciousness, since this nullity of the object is precisely the *self-confirmation* of the non-objectivity, of the *abstraction* of itself. For *consciousness itself* the nullity of the object has a positive meaning because it *knows* this nullity, the objective being, as *its self-alienation;* because it knows that it exists only as a result of its own self-alienation....

The way in which consciousness is, and in which something is for it, is *knowing*. Knowing is its sole act. Something therefore comes to be for consciousness insofar as the latter *knows* this *something*. Knowing is its sole objective relation. Consciousness, then, knows the nullity of the object (i.e., knows the non-existence of the distinction between the object and itself, the non-existence of the object for it) because it knows the object as its *self-alienation;* that is, it knows itself—knows knowing as object—because the object is only the *semblance* of an object, a piece of mystification, which in its essence, however, is nothing else but knowing itself, which has confronted itself with itself and hence has confronted itself with a *nullity*—a something which has *no* objectivity outside the knowing. Or: knowing knows that in relating itself to an object it is only *outside* itself—that it only externalizes itself; that *it itself* only *appears* to itself as an object—or that that which appears to it as an object is only itself.

On the other hand, says Hegel, there is here at the same time this other moment, that consciousness has just as much annulled and reabsorbed this externalization and objectivity, being thus *at home* in its *other-being as such.*

In this discussion all the illusions of speculation are brought together.

First of all: consciousness, self-consciousness, is *at home* in *its other-being as such.* It is therefore—or if we here abstract from the Hegelian abstraction and put the self-consciousness of man instead of self-consciousness—it is *at home* in its *other being as such.* This implies, for one thing, that consciousness (knowing as knowing, thinking as thinking) pretends to be directly the *other* of itself—to be the world of sense, the real world, life—thought surpassing itself in thought (Feuerbach).[57] This aspect is contained herein, inasmuch as consciousness as mere consciousness takes offence not at estranged objectivity, but at *objectivity as such.*

Secondly, this implies that self-conscious man, insofar as he has recognised and superseded the spiritual world (or his world's spiritual, general mode of being) as self-alienation, nevertheless again confirms it in this alienated shape and passes it off as his true mode of being—re-establishes it, and pretends to be *at home in his other-being as such.* Thus, for instance, after superseding religion, after recognising religion to be a product of self-alienation he yet finds confirmation of himself in *religion as religion.* Here *is* the root of Hegel's *false* positivism, or of his merely *apparent* criticism: this is what Feuerbach designated as the positing, negating and re-establishing of religion or theology—but it has to be expressed in more general terms. Thus reason is at home in unreason as unreason. The man who has recognised that he is leading an alienated life in law, politics, etc., is leading his true human life in this alienated life as such. Self-affirmation, self-confirmation *in contradiction* with itself—in contradiction both with the knowledge of and with the essential being of the object—is thus true *knowledge* and *life.*

There can therefore no longer be any question about an act of accommodation on Hegel's part *vis-à-vis* religion, the state, etc., since this lie is the lie of his principle.

If I *know* religion as *alienated* human self-consciousness, then what I know in it as religion is not my self-consciousness, but my alienated self-consciousness confirmed in it. I therefore know my self-consciousness that belongs to itself, to its very nature, confirmed not in *religion* but rather in *annihilated* and *superseded* religion.

In Hegel, therefore, the negation of the negation is not the confirmation of the true essence, effected precisely through negation of the pseudo-essence. With him the negation of the negation is the confirmation of the pseudo-essence, or of the self-

---

[57] Marx refers to § 30 of Feuerbach's *Grundsätze der Philosophie der Zukunft,* which says: "Hegel is a thinker who *surpasses* himself in thinking."

estranged essence in its denial; or it is the denial of this pseudo-essence as an objective being dwelling outside man and independent of him, and its transformation into the subject.

A peculiar role, therefore, is played by the act of *superseding* in which denial and preservation, i.e., affirmation, are bound together.

Thus, for example, in Hegel's philosophy of law, *civil law* superseded equals *morality*, morality superseded equals the *family*, the family superseded equals *civil society*, civil society superseded equals the *state*, the state superseded equals *world history*. In the *actual world* civil law, morality, the family, civil society, the state, etc., remain in existence, only they have become *moments*—states of the existence and being of man—which have no validity in isolation, but dissolve and engender one another, etc. They have become *moments of motion*.

In their actual existence this *mobile* nature of theirs is hidden. It appears and is made manifest only in thought, in philosophy. Hence my true religious existence is my existence in the *philosophy of religion;* my true political existence is my existence in the *philosophy of law;* my true natural existence, existence in the *philosophy of nature;* my true artistic existence, existence in the *philosophy of art;* my true *human* existence, my *existence in philosophy*. Likewise the true existence of religion, the state, nature, art, is the *philosophy* of religion, of nature, of the state and of art. If, however, the philosophy of religion, etc., is for me the sole true existence of religion then, too, it is only as a *philosopher of religion* that I am truly religious, and so I deny *real* religious sentiment and the really *religious* man. But at the same time I *assert* them, in part within my own existence or within the alien existence which I oppose to them—for this *is* only their *philosophic* expression—and in part I assert them in their distinct original shape, since for me they represent merely the *apparent* other-being, allegories, forms of their own true existence (i.e., of my *philosophical* existence) hidden under sensuous disguises.

In just the same way, *quality* superseded equals *quantity*, quantity superseded equals *measure*, measure superseded equals *essence*, essence superseded equals *appearance*, appearance superseded equals *actuality*, actuality superseded equals the *concept*, the concept superseded equals *objectivity*, objectivity superseded equals the *absolute idea*, the absolute idea superseded equals *nature*, nature superseded equals *subjective* mind, subjective mind superseded equals *ethical* objective mind, ethical mind superseded equals *art*, art superseded equals *religion*, religion superseded equals *absolute knowledge*.[58]

On the one hand, this act of superseding is a transcending of a conceptual entity; thus, private property *as a concept* is transcended in the *concept* of morality. And because thought imagines itself to be directly the other of itself, to be *sensuous reality*—and therefore takes its own action for *sensuous, real* action—this superseding in thought, which leaves its object in existence in the real world, believes that it has really overcome it. On the other hand, because the object has now become for it a moment of thought, thought takes it in its reality too to be self-confirmation of itself—of self-consciousness, of abstraction.

From the one point of view the entity which Hegel *supersedes* in philosophy is therefore not *real* religion, the *real* state, or *real* nature, but religion itself already as an object of knowledge, i.e., *dogmatics;* the same with *jurisprudence, political science* and

---

[58] This enumeration gives the major categories of Hegel's *Encyclopädie der philosophischen Wissenschaften* in the order in which they are examined by Hegel. Similarly, the categories reproduced by Marx above (on p. 149), from "civil law" to "world history," are given in the order in which they appear in Hegel's *Philosophie des Rechts*.

natural science. From the one point of view, therefore, he stands in opposition both to the *real* thing and to immediate, unphilosophic *science* or the unphilosophic *conceptions* of this thing. He therefore contradicts their conventional conceptions.[59]

On the other hand, the religious, etc., man can find in Hegel his final confirmation.

It is now time to formulate the *positive* aspects of the Hegelian dialectic within the realm of estrangement.

(a) *Supersession* as an objective movement of *retracting* the alienation *into self.* This is the insight, expressed within the estrangement, concerning the *appropriation* of the objective essence through the supersession of its estrangement; it is the estranged insight into the *real objectification* of man, into the real appropriation of his objective essence through the annihilation of the *estranged* character of the objective world, through the supersession of the objective world in its estranged mode of being. In the same way atheism, being the supersession of God, is the advent of theoretic humanism, and communism, as the supersession of private property, is the vindication of real human life as man's possession and thus the advent of practical humanism, or atheism is humanism mediated with itself through the supersession of religion, whilst communism is humanism mediated with itself through the supersession of private property. Only through the supersession of this mediation—which is itself, however, a necessary premise—does positively self-deriving humanism, *positive* humanism, come into being.

But atheism and communism are no flight, no abstraction, no loss of the objective world created by man—of man's essential powers born to the realm of objectivity; they are not a returning in poverty to unnatural, primitive simplicity. On the contrary, they are but the first real emergence, the actual realization for man of man's essence and of his essence as something real.

Thus, by grasping the *positive* meaning of self-referred negation (although again in estranged fashion) Hegel grasps man's self-estrangement, the alienation of man's essence, man's loss of objectivity and his loss of realness as self-discovery, manifestation of his nature, objectification and realization. In short, within the sphere of abstraction, Hegel conceives labour as man's act of *self-genesis*—conceives man's relation to himself as an alien being and the manifestation of himself as an alien being to be the emergence of *species-consciousness* and *species-life.*

(b) However, apart from, or rather in consequence of, the referral already described, this act appears in Hegel:

First as a *merely formal,* because abstract, act, because the human being itself is taken to be only an *abstract, thinking being,* conceived merely as self-consciousness. And,

Secondly, because the exposition is *formal* and *abstract,* the supersession of the alienation becomes a confirmation of the alienation; or for Hegel this movement of *self-genesis* and *self-objectification* in the form of *self-alienation and self-estrangement* is the *absolute,* and hence final, *expression of human life*—of life with itself as its aim, of life at peace with itself, and in unity with its essence.

This movement, in its abstract form as dialectic, is therefore regarded as *truly human life,* and because it is nevertheless an abstraction—an estrangement of human life—it is regarded as a *divine process,* but as the divine process of man, a process traversed by man's abstract, pure, absolute essence that is distinct from himself.

Thirdly, this process must have a bearer, a subject. But the subject only comes into

---

[59] The conventional conception of theology, jurisprudence, political science, natural science, etc.—*Ed.*

being as a result. This result—the subject knowing itself as absolute self-consciousness—is therefore *God, absolute Spirit, the self-knowing and self-manifesting idea.* Real man and real nature become mere predicates—symbols of this hidden, unreal man and of this unreal nature. Subject and predicate are therefore related to each other in absolute reversal—a *mystical subject-object* or a *subjectivity reaching beyond the object*—the *absolute subject* as a *process,* as *subject alienating* itself and returning from alienation into itself, but at the same time retracting this alienation into itself, and the subject as this process; a pure, *incessant* revolving within itself.

   First, Formal and abstract conception of man's act of self-creation or self-objectification.

   Hegel having posited man as equivalent to self-consciousness, the estranged object—the estranged essential reality of man—is nothing but *consciousness, the thought of* estrangement merely—estrangement's *abstract* and therefore empty and unreal expression, *negation.* The supersession of the alienation is therefore likewise nothing but an abstract, empty supersession of that empty abstraction—the *negation of the negation.* The rich, living, sensuous, concrete activity of self-objectification is therefore reduced to its mere abstraction, *absolute negativity*—an abstraction which is again fixed as such and considered as an independent activity—as sheer activity. Because this so-called negativity is nothing but the *abstract, empty* form of that real living act, its content can in consequence be merely a *formal* content produced by abstraction from all content. As a result therefore one gets general, abstract *forms of abstraction* pertaining to every content and on that account indifferent to, and, consequently, valid for, all content—the thought-forms or logical categories torn from *real* mind and from *real* nature. (We shall unfold the *logical* content of absolute negativity further on.)

   Hegel's positive achievement here, in his speculative logic, is that the *definite concepts,* the universal *fixed thought-forms* in their independence *vis-à-vis* nature and mind are a necessary result of the general estrangement of the human being and therefore also of a human thought, and that Hegel has therefore brought these together and presented them as moments of the abstraction-process. For example, superseded being is essence, superseded essence is concept, the concept superseded is ... absolute idea. But what, then, is the absolute idea? It supersedes its own self again, if it does not want to traverse once more from the beginning the whole act of abstraction, and to satisfy itself with being a totality of abstractions or the self-comprehending abstraction. But abstraction comprehending itself as abstraction knows itself to be nothing: it must abandon itself—abandon abstraction—and so it arrives at an entity which is its exact opposite—at *nature.* Thus, the entire logic is the demonstration that abstract thought is nothing in itself; that the absolute idea is nothing for itself; that only *nature is* something.

   The absolute idea, the abstract idea, which "*considered* with regard to its unity with itself is *intuiting* (*Logic* § 244), and which "in its own absolute truth *resolves* to let the moment of its particularity or of initial characterization and other-being, the *immediate idea,* as its reflection, *go forth* freely *from itself as nature*" (loc. cit.)—this whole idea which behaves in such a strange and bizarre way, and which has given the Hegelians such terrible headaches, is from beginning to end nothing else but *abstraction* (i.e., the abstract thinker), which, made wise by experience and enlightened concerning its truth, resolves under various (false and themselves still abstract) conditions to *abandon itself* and to replace its self-absorption, nothingness, generality and indeterminateness by its other-being, the particular, and the determinate; resolves to let *nature,* which it held hidden in itself only as an abstraction, as a thought-entity, *go forth freely from itself;* that is to say, this idea resolves to forsake abstraction and to have a look at nature *free* of abstraction. The abstract idea, which without mediation becomes *intuiting*, is indeed nothing else but abstract thinking that gives itself up and resolves on *intuition*. This entire transition from logic to natural philosophy is nothing else but the transition—so difficult to effect for the abstract thinker, who therefore describes it in such an adventurous way—from *abstracting* to *intuiting*. The *mystical* feeling which drives the philosopher forward from abstract thinking to intuiting is *boredom*—the longing for content.

(The man estranged from himself is also the thinker estranged from his *essence*—that is, from the natural and human essence. His thoughts are therefore fixed mental forms dwelling outside nature and man. Hegel has locked up all these fixed mental forms together in his logic, interpreting each of them first as negation—that is, as an *alienation* of *human* thought—and then as negation of the negation—that is, as a superseding of this alienation, as a *real* expression of human thought. But as this still takes place within the confines of the estrangement, this negation of the negation is in part the restoring of these fixed forms in their estrangement; in part a stopping at the last act—the act of self-reference in alienation—as the true mode of being of these fixed mental forms;[60] and in part, to the extent that this abstraction apprehends itself and experiences an infinite weariness with itself, there makes its appearance in Hegel, in the form of the resolution to recognise *nature* as the essential being and to go over to intuition, the abandonment of abstract thought—the abandonment of thought revolving solely within the orbit of thought, of thought *sans* eyes, *sans* teeth, *sans* ears, *sans* everything.)

But *nature* too, taken abstractly, for itself—nature fixed in isolation from man—is *nothing* for man. It goes without saying that the abstract thinker who has committed himself to intuiting, intuits nature abstractly. Just as nature lay enclosed in the thinker in the form of the absolute idea, in the form of a thought-entity—in a shape which was obscure and enigmatic even to him—so by letting it emerge from himself he has really let emerge only this *abstract nature,* only nature as a *thought-entity*—but now with the significance that it is the other-being of thought, that it is real, intuited nature—nature distinguished from abstract thought. Or, to talk in human language, the abstract thinker learns in his intuition of nature that the entities which he thought to create from nothing, from pure abstraction—the entities he believed he was producing in the divine dialectic as pure products of the labour of thought, forever shuttling back and forth in itself and never looking outward into reality—are nothing else but *abstractions* from *characteristics of nature.* To him, therefore, the whole of nature merely repeats the logical abstractions in a sensuous, external form. He once more *resolves* nature into these abstractions. Thus, his intuition of nature is only the act of confirming his abstraction from the intuition of nature—is only the conscious repetition by him of the process of creating his abstraction. Thus, for example, time equals negativity referred to itself (Hegel, *Encyclopädie der philosophischen Wissenschaften im Grundrisse.* p. 238). To the superseded becoming as being there corresponds, in natural form, superseded movement as matter. Light is *reflection-in-itself*, the *natural* form. Body as *moon* and *comet* is the *natural* form of the *antithesis* which according to logic is on the one side the *positive*

---

[60] This means that what Hegel does is to put in place of these fixed abstractions the act of abstraction which revolves in its own circle. We must therefore give him the credit for having indicated the source of all these inappropriate concepts which originally appertained to particular philosophers; for having brought them together; and for having created the entire compass of abstraction as the object of criticism, instead of some specific abstraction.) (Why Hegel separates thought from the *subject* we shall see later; at this stage it is already clear, however, that when man is not, his characteristic expression cannot be human either, and so neither could thought be grasped as an expression of man as a human and natural subject endowed with eyes, ears, etc., and living in society, in the world, and in nature.

resting on itself and on the other side the *negative* resting on itself. The earth is the *natural* form of the logical *ground,* as the negative unity of the antithesis, etc.

Nature as nature—that is to say, insofar as it is still sensuously distinguished from that secret sense hidden within it—nature isolated, distinguished from these abstractions is *nothing*—a *nothing proving itself to be nothing*—is *devoid of sense,* or has only the sense of being an externality which has to be annulled.

"In the finite-*teleological* position is to be found the correct premise that nature does not contain within itself the absolute purpose." (p. 225).

Its purpose is the confirmation of abstraction.

"Nature has shown itself to be the idea in the *form of other-being.* Since the *idea* is in this form the negative of itself or *external to itself,* nature is not just relatively external *vis-à-vis* this idea, but *externality* constitutes the form in which it exists as nature." (p. 227).

Externality here is not to be understood as the *world of sense* which *manifests itself* and is accessible to the light, to the man endowed with senses. It is to be taken here in the sense of alienation, of a mistake, a defect, which ought not to be. For what is true is still the idea. Nature is only the *form* of the idea's *other-being.* And since abstract thought is the *essence,* that which is external to it is by its essence something merely *external.* The abstract thinker recognizes at the same time that *sensuousness—externality* in contrast to thought shuttling back and forth *within itself*—is the essence of nature. But he expresses this contrast in such a way as to make this *externality of nature*, its *contrast* to thought, its *defect,* so that inasmuch as it is distinguished from abstraction, nature is something defective. An entity which is defective not merely for me or in my eyes but in itself— intrinsically—has something outside itself which it lacks. That is, its essence is different from it itself. Nature has therefore to supersede itself for the abstract thinker, for it is already posited by him as a potentially *superseded* being.

"For us, mind has *nature* for its *premise,* being nature's *truth* and for that reason its *absolute prius.* In this truth nature *has vanished,* and mind has resulted as the idea arrived at being-for-itself, the *object* of which, as well as the *subject,* is the *concept.* This identity is *absolute negativity,* for whereas in nature the concept has its perfect external objectivity, this its alienation has been superseded, and in this alienation the concept has become identical with itself. But it is this identity therefore, only in being a return out of nature." (p. 392).

"As the *abstract* idea, *revelation* is unmediated transition to, the *coming-to-be* of, nature; as the revelation of the mind, which is free, it is the *positing* of nature as the *mind's* world—a positing which, being reflection, is at the same time, a *presupposing* of the world as independently existing nature. Revelation in conception is the creation of nature as the mind's being, in which the mind procures the *affirmation* and the *truth* of its freedom." *"The absolute is mind.* This is the highest definition of the absolute."

APPENDIX

OUTLINES OF A CRITIQUE OF POLITICAL ECONOMY

By Frederick Engels

Political economy came into being as a natural result of the expansion of trade, and with its appearance elementary, unscientific huckstering was replaced by a developed system of licensed fraud, an entire science of enrichment.

This political economy or science of enrichment born of the merchants' mutual envy and greed, bears on its brow the mark of the most detestable selfishness. People still lived in the naive belief that gold and silver were wealth, and therefore considered nothing more urgent than the prohibition everywhere of the export of the "precious" metals. The nations faced each other like misers, each clasping to himself with both arms his precious money-bag, eyeing his neighbours with envy and distrust. Every conceivable means was employed to lure from the nations with whom one had commerce as much ready cash as possible, and to retain snugly within the customs-boundary all which had happily been gathered in.

If this principle had been rigorously carried through trade would have been killed. People therefore began to go beyond this first stage. They came to appreciate that capital locked up in a chest was dead capital, while capital in circulation increased continuously. They then became more sociable, sent off their ducats as call-birds to bring others back with them, and realised that there is no harm in paying A too much for his commodity so long as it can be disposed of to B at a higher price.

On this basis the *Mercantile System* was built. The avaricious character of trade was to some extent already beginning to be hidden. The nations drew slightly nearer to one another, concluded trade and friendship agreements, did business with one another and, for the sake of larger profits, treated one another with all possible love and kindness. But in fact there was still the old avarice and selfishness and from time to time this erupted in wars, which in that day were all based on trade jealousy. In these wars it also became evident that trade, like robbery, is based on the law of the strong hand. No scruples whatever were felt about exacting by cunning or violence such treaties as were held to be the most advantageous.

The cardinal point in the whole Mercantile System is the theory of the balance of trade. For as it still subscribed to the dictum that gold and silver constitute wealth, only such transactions as would finally bring ready cash into the country were considered profitable. To ascertain this, exports were compared with imports. When more had been exported than imported, it was believed that the difference had come into the country in ready cash, and that the country was richer by that difference. The art of the economists, therefore, consisted in ensuring that at the end of each year exports should show a favourable balance over imports; and for the sake of this ridiculous illusion thousands of men have been slaughtered! Trade, too, has had its crusades and inquisitions.

The eighteenth century, the century of revolution, also revolutionised economics. But just as all the revolutions of this century were one-sided and bogged down in antitheses—just as abstract materialism was set in opposition to abstract spiritualism, the republic to monarchy, the social contract to divine right—likewise the economic revolution did not get beyond antithesis. The premises remained everywhere in force: materialism did not attack the Christian contempt for and humiliation of Man, and merely posited Nature instead of the Christian God as the Absolute confronting Man. In politics no one dreamt of examining the premises of the state as such. It did not occur to economics to question the *validity of private property*. Therefore, the new economics was only half an advance. It was obliged to betray and to disavow its own premises, to have recourse to sophistry and hypocrisy so as to cover up the contradictions in which it became entangled, so as to reach the conclusions to which it was driven not by its premises but by the humane spirit of the century. Thus economics took on a philanthropic character. It withdrew its favour from the producers and bestowed it on the consumers. It affected a solemn abhorrence of the bloody terror of the Mercantile System, and proclaimed trade to be a bond of friendship and union among nations as among individuals. All was pure splendour and magnificence—yet the premises reasserted themselves soon enough, and in contrast to this sham philanthropy produced the Malthusian population theory—the crudest, most barbarous theory that ever existed, a system of despair which struck down all those beautiful phrases about philanthropy and world citizenship. The premises begot and reared the factory system and modern slavery, which yields nothing in inhumanity and cruelty to ancient slavery. Modern economics—the system of free trade based on Adam Smith's *Wealth of Nations*—reveals itself to be that same hypocrisy, inconsistency and immorality which now confront free humanity in every sphere.

But was Smith's system, then, not an advance? Of course it was, and a necessary advance at that. It was necessary to overthrow the mercantile system with its monopolies and hindrances to trade, so that the true consequences of private property could come to light. It was necessary for all these petty, local and national considerations to recede into the background, so that the struggle of our time could become a universal human struggle. It was necessary for the theory of private property to leave the purely empirical path of merely objective inquiry and to acquire a more scientific character which would also make it responsible for the consequences, and thus transfer the matter to a universally human sphere. It was necessary to carry the immorality contained in the old economics to its highest pitch, by attempting to deny it and by the hypocrisy introduced (a necessary result of that attempt). All this lay in the nature of the case. We gladly concede that it is only the justification and accomplishment of free trade that has enabled us to go beyond the economics of private property; but we must at the same time have the right to expose the utter theoretical and practical nullity of this free trade.

The nearer to our time the economists whom we have to judge, the more severe must our judgment become. For while Smith and Malthus found only scattered fragments, the modern economists had the whole system complete before them: the consequences had all been drawn; the contradictions came clearly enough to light; yet they did not come to examining the premises, and still accepted the responsibility for the whole system. The nearer the economists come to the present time, the further they depart from honesty. With every advance of time, sophistry necessarily increases, so as to prevent economics from lagging behind the times. This is why *Ricardo*, for instance, is more guilty than *Adam Smith*, and *McCulloch* and *Mill* more guilty than *Ricardo*.

Even the Mercantile System cannot be correctly judged by modern economics since the latter is itself one-sided and as yet burdened with that very system's premises. Only that view which rises above the opposition of the two systems, which criticises the premises common to both and proceeds from a purely human, universal basis, can assign to both their proper position. It will become evident that the protagonists of free trade are more inveterate monopolists than the old Mercantilists themselves. It will become evident that the sham humanity of the modern economists hides a barbarism of which their predecessors knew nothing; that the older economists' conceptual confusion is simple and consistent compared with the double-tongued logic of their attackers, and that neither of the two factions can reproach the other with anything which would not recoil upon themselves.

This is why modern liberal economics cannot comprehend the restoration of the Mercantile System by List, whilst for us the matter is quite simple. The inconsistency and ambiguity of liberal economics must of necessity dissolve again into its basic components. Just as theology must either regress to blind faith or progress towards free philosophy, free trade must produce the restoration of monopolies on the one hand and the abolition of private property on the other.

The only *positive* advance which liberal economics has made is the elaboration of the laws of private property. These are contained in it, at any rate, although not yet fully elaborated and clearly expressed. It follows that on all points where it is a question of deciding which is the shortest road to wealth—i. e., in all strictly economic controversies—the protagonists of free trade have right on their side. That is, needless to say, in controversies with the monopolists—not with the opponents of private property, for the English Socialists have long since proved both practically and theoretically that the latter are in a position to settle economic questions more correctly even from an economic point of view.

In the critique of political economy, therefore, we shall examine the basic categories, uncover the contradiction introduced by the free-trade system, and bring out the consequences of both sides of the contradiction.

The term "national wealth" has only arisen as a result of the liberal economists' passion for generalization. As long as private property exists, this term has no meaning. The "national wealth" of the English is very great and yet they are the poorest people under the sun. One must either discard this term completely, or accept such premises as give it meaning. Similarly with the terms "national economy" and "political or public economy." In the present circumstances that science ought to be called *private* economy, for its public connections exist only for the sake of private property.

The immediate consequence of private property is *trade*—exchange of reciprocal requirements—buying and selling. This trade, like every activity, must under the dominion of private property become a direct source of gain for the trader, i.e., each must seek to sell as dear as possible and buy as cheap as possible. In every purchase and sale, therefore, two men with diametrically opposed interests confront each other. The confrontation is decidedly antagonistic, for each knows the intentions of the other—knows that they are opposed to his own. Therefore, the first consequence is mutual mistrust, on the one hand, and the justification of this mistrust—the application of immoral means to attain an immoral end—on the other. Thus, the first maxim in trade is secretiveness—the concealment of everything which might reduce the value of the article in question. The result is that in trade it is permitted to take the utmost advantage of the ignorance, the trust, of the opposing party, and likewise to impute qualities to one's commodity which it does not possess. In a word, trade is legalised fraud. Any merchant who wants to give truth its due can bear me witness that actual practice conforms with this theory.

The Mercantile System still had a certain artless Catholic candour and did not in the least conceal the immoral nature of trade. We have seen how it openly paraded its mean avarice. The mutually hostile attitude of the nations in the eighteenth century, loathsome envy and trade jealousy, were the logical consequences of trade as such. Public opinion had not yet become humanised. Why, therefore, conceal things which resulted from the inhuman, hostile nature of trade itself?

But when the *economic Luther*, Adam Smith, criticised past economics things had changed considerably. The century had been humanised; reason had asserted itself, morality began to claim its eternal right. The extorted trade treaties, the commercial wars, the strict isolation of the nations, offended too greatly against advanced consciousness. Protestant hypocrisy took the place of Catholic candour. Smith proved that humanity, too, was rooted in the nature of commerce; that commerce must become "among nations, as among individuals, a bond of union and friendship" instead of being "the most fertile source of discord and animosity" (cf. *Wealth of Nations*, Bk. 4, Ch. 3, § 2); that after all it lay in the nature of things for trade, taken overall, to be advantageous to *all* parties concerned.

Smith was right to eulogise trade as humane. There is nothing absolutely immoral in the world. Trade, too, has an aspect wherein it pays homage to morality and humanity. But what homage! The law of the strong hand, the open highway robbery of the Middle Ages, became humanised when it passed over into trade; and trade became humanised when its first stage characterised by the prohibition of the export of money passed over into the Mercantile System. Then the Mercantile System itself was humanised. Naturally, it is in the interest of the trader to be on good terms with the one from whom he buys cheap as well as with the other to whom he sells dear. A nation therefore acts very imprudently if it fosters feelings of animosity in its suppliers and customers. The more friendly, the more advantageous. Such is the humanity of trade. And this hypocritical way of misusing morality for immoral purposes is the pride of the free-trade system.

"Have we not overthrown the barbarism of the monopolies?" exclaim the hypocrites. "Have we not carried civilisation to distant parts of the world? Have we not brought about the fraternisation of the peoples, and reduced the number of wars?" Yes, all this you have done—but *how!* You have destroyed the small monopolies so that the *one* great basic monopoly, property, may function the more freely and unrestrictedly. You have civilised the ends of the earth to win new terrain for the deployment of your vile avarice. You have brought about the fraternisation of the peoples—but the fraternity is the fraternity of thieves. You have reduced the number of wars—to earn all the bigger profits in peace, to intensify to the utmost the enmity between individuals, the ignominious war of competition! When have you done anything out of pure humanity, from consciousness of the futility of the opposition between the general and the individual interest? When have you been moral without being interested, without harbouring at the back of your mind immoral, egoistical motives?

By dissolving nationalities, the liberal economic system had done its best to universalise enmity, to transform mankind into a horde of ravenous beasts (for what else are competitors?) who devour one another just *because* each has identical interests with all the others—after this preparatory work there remained but one step to take before the goal was reached, the dissolution of the family.

To accomplish this, economy's own beautiful invention, the factory system, came to its aid. The last vestige of common interests, the community of goods in the possession of the family, has been undermined by the factory system and—at least here in England—is already in the process of dissolution. It is a common practice for children, as soon as they are capable of work (i.e., as soon as they reach the age of nine), to spend their wages themselves, to look upon their parental home as a mere boarding-house, and hand over to their parents a fixed amount for food and lodging. How can it be otherwise? What else can result from the separation of interests, such as forms the basis of the free-trade system? Once a principle is set in motion, it works by its own impetus through all its consequences, whether the economists like it or not.

But the economist does not know himself what cause he serves. He does not know that with all his egoistical reasoning he nevertheless forms but a link in the chain of mankind's universal progress. He does not know that by his dissolution of all sectional interests he merely paves the way for the great transformation to which the century is moving—the reconciliation of mankind with nature and with itself.

The next category established by trade is *value*. There is no dispute between the old and the modern economists over this category, just as there is none over all the others, since the monopolists in their obsessive mania for getting rich had no time left to concern themselves with categories. All controversies over such points stem from the modern economists.

The economist who lives by antitheses has also of course a *double* value—abstract or real value and exchange-value. There was a protracted quarrel over the nature of real value between the English, who defined the costs of production as the expression of real value, and the Frenchman Say, who claimed to measure this value by the utility of an object. The quarrel hung in doubt from the beginning of the century, then became dormant without a decision having been reached. The economists cannot decide anything.

The English—McCulloch and Ricardo in particular—thus assert that the abstract value of a thing is determined by the costs of production. *Nota bene* the abstract value, not the exchangevalue, the *"exchangeable value,"*[61] value in exchange—that, they say, is something quite different. Why are the costs of production the measure of value? Because—listen to this!—because no one in ordinary conditions and leaving aside the circumstance of competition would sell an object for less than it costs him to produce it. Would sell? What have we to do with "selling" here, where it is not a question of value in *exchange*? So we find trade again, which we are specifically supposed to leave aside—and what trade! A trade in which the cardinal factor, the circumstance of competition, is not to be taken into account! First, an abstract value; now also an abstract trade—a trade without competition, i.e., a man without a body, a thought without a brain to produce thoughts. And does the economist never stop to think that as soon as competition is left out of account there is no guarantee at all that the producer will sell his commodity just at the cost of production? What confusion!

Furthermore: Let us concede for a moment that everything is as the economist says. Supposing someone were to make with tremendous exertion and at enormous cost something utterly useless, something which no one desires—is that also worth its production costs? Certainly not, says the economist: Who will want to buy it? So we suddenly have not only Say's much decried utility but alongside it—with "buying"—the circumstance of competition. It can't be done—the economist cannot for one moment hold on to his abstraction. Not only what he painfully seeks to remove—competition—

---

[61] English term quoted by Engels.—Ed.

but also what he attacks—utility—crops up at every moment. Abstract value and its determination by the costs of production are, after all, only abstractions, nonentities.

But let us suppose once more for a moment that the economist is correct—how then will he determine the costs of production without taking account of competition? When examining the costs of production we shall see that this category too is based on competition, and here once more it becomes evident how little the economist is able to substantiate his claims.

If we turn to Say, we find the same abstraction. The utility of an object is something purely subjective, something which cannot be decided absolutely, and certainly something which cannot be decided at least as long as one still roams about in antitheses. According to this theory, the necessities of life ought to possess more value than luxury articles. The only possible way to arrive at a more or less objective, *apparently* general decision on the greater or lesser utility of an object is, under the dominion of private property, by competition; and yet it is precisely that circumstance which is to be left aside. But if competition is admitted production costs come in as well; for no one will sell for less than what he has himself invested in production. Thus, here, too, the one side of the opposition passes over involuntarily into the other.

Let us try to introduce clarity into this confusion. The value of an object includes both factors, which the contending parties arbitrarily separate—and, as we have seen, unsuccessfully. Value is the relation of production costs to utility. The first application of value is the decision as to whether a thing ought to be produced at all; i.e., as to whether utility counterbalances production costs. Only then can one talk of the application of value to exchange. The production costs of two objects being equal, the deciding factor determining their comparative value will be utility.

This basis is the only just basis of exchange. But if one proceeds from this basis, who is to decide the utility of the object? The mere opinion of the parties concerned? Then in any event *one* will be cheated. Or are we to assume a determination grounded in the inherent utility of the object independent of the parties concerned, and not apparent to them? If so, the exchange can only be effected by *coercion*, and each party considers itself cheated. The contradiction between the real inherent utility of the thing and the determination of that utility, between the determination of utility and the freedom of those who exchange, cannot be superseded without superseding private property; and once this is superseded, there can no longer be any question of exchange as it exists at present. The practical application of the concept of value will then be increasingly confined to the decision about production, and that is its proper sphere.

But how do matters stand at present? We have seen that the concept of value is violently torn asunder, and that each of the separate sides is declared to be the whole. Production costs, distorted from the outset by competition, are supposed to be value itself. So is mere subjective utility—since no other kind of utility can exist at present. To help these lame definitions on to their feet, it is in both cases necessary to have recourse to competition; and the best of it is that with the English competition represents utility, in contrast to the costs of production, whilst inversely with Say it introduces the costs of production in contrast to utility. But what kind of utility, what kind of production costs, does it introduce? Its utility depends on chance, on fashion, on the whim of the rich; its production costs fluctuate with the fortuitous relationship of demand and supply.

The difference between real value and exchange-value is based on a fact—namely, that the value of a thing differs from the so-called equivalent given for it in trade; i.e., that this equivalent is not an equivalent. This so-called equivalent is the *price* of the thing, and if the economist were honest, he would employ this term for "value in exchange." But he has still to keep up some sort of pretence that price is somehow bound up with value, lest the immorality of trade become too obvious. It is, however, quite correct, and a fundamental law of private property, that *price* is determined by the reciprocal action of production costs and competition. This purely empirical law was the first to be discovered by the economist; and from this law he then abstracted his "real value," i.e., the price at the time when competition is in a state of equilibrium, when demand and supply cover each other. Then, of course, what remains over are the costs of production and it is these which the economist proceeds to call "real value," whereas it is merely a definite aspect of price. Thus everything in economics stands on its head. Value, the primary factor, the source of price, is made dependent on price, its own product. As is well known, this inversion is the essence of abstraction; on which see Feuerbach.

According to the economists, the production costs of a commodity consist of three elements: the rent for the piece of land required to produce the raw material; the capital with its profit, and the wages for the labour required for production and manufacture. But it becomes immediately evident that capital and labour are identical, since the economists themselves confess that capital is "stored-up labour." We are therefore left with only two sides—the natural, objective side, land; and the human, subjective side, labour, which includes capital and, besides capital, a third factor which the economist does not think about—I mean the mental element of invention, of thought, alongside the physical element of sheer labour. What has the economist to do with inventiveness? Have not all inventions fallen into his lap without any effort on his part? Has *one* of them cost him anything? Why then should he bother about them in the calculation of production costs? Land, capital and labour are for him the conditions of wealth, and he requires nothing else. Science is no concern of his. What does it matter to him that he has received its gifts through Berthollet, Davy, Liebig, Watt, Cartwright, etc.—gifts which have benefited him and his production immeasurably? He does not know how to calculate such things; the advances of science go beyond his figures. But in a rational order which has gone beyond the division of interests as it is found with the economist, the mental element certainly belongs among the elements of production and will find its place, too, in economics among the costs of production. And here it is certainly gratifying to know that the promotion of science also brings its material reward; to know that a single achievement of science like James Watt's steam-engine has brought in more for the world in the first fifty years of its existence than the world has spent on the promotion of science since the beginning of time.

We have, then, two elements of production in operation—nature and man, with man again active physically and mentally, and can now return to the economist and his production costs.

What cannot be monopolised has no value, says the economist—a proposition which we shall examine more closely later on. If we say "has no *price*", then the proposition is valid for the order which rests on private property. If land could be had as easily as air, no one would pay rent. Since this is not the case, but since, rather, the extent of a piece of land to be appropriated is limited in any particular case, one pays rent for the appropriated, i.e., the monopolised land, or one pays down a purchase price for it. After this enlightenment about the origin of the value of land it is, however, very strange to have to hear from the economist that the rent of land is the difference between the yield from the land for which rent is paid and from the worst land worth cultivating at all. As is well known, this is the definition of rent fully developed for the first time by Ricardo. This definition is indeed correct in practice if one presupposes that a fall in demand reacts *instantaneously* on rent, and at once puts a corresponding amount of the worst cultivated land out of cultivation. This, however, is not the case, and the definition is therefore inadequate. Moreover, it does not cover the causation of rent, and is therefore even for that reason untenable. In opposition to this definition, Col. T. P. Thompson, the champion of the AntiCorn Law League, revived Adam Smith's definition, and substantiated it. According to him, rent is the relation between the competition of those striving for the use of the land and the limited quantity of available land. Here at least is a return to the origin of rent; but this explanation does not take into account the varying fertility of the soil, just as the previous explanation leaves out competition.

Once more, therefore we have two one-sided and hence only partial definitions of a single object. As in the case of the concept of value, we shall again have to combine these two definitions so as to find the correct definition which follows from the development of the thing itself and thus embraces all practice. Rent is the relation between the productivity of the land, the natural side (which in turn consists of *natural* fertility and *human* cultivation—labour applied to effect improvement), and the human side, competition. The economists may shake their heads over this "definition"; they will discover to their horror that it embraces everything relevant to this matter.

The *landowner* has nothing with which to reproach the merchant.

He practices robbery in monopolising the land. He practices robbery in exploiting for his own benefit the increase in population which increases competition and thus the value of his estate; in turning into a source of personal advantage that which has not been his own doing—that which is his by sheer accident. He practices robbery in *leasing his land*, when he eventually seizes for himself the improvements effected by his tenant. This is the secret of the ever-increasing wealth of the big landowners.

The axioms which qualify as robbery the landowner's method of deriving an income—namely, that each has a right to the product of his labour, or that no one shall reap where he has not sown—are not advanced by us. The first excludes the duty of feeding children; the second deprives each generation of the right to live, since each generation starts with what it inherits from the preceding generation. These axioms are, rather, consequences of private property. One should either put into effect the consequences or abandon private property as a premise.

Indeed, the original act of appropriation itself is justified by the assertion of the still earlier existence of *common* property rights. Thus, wherever we turn, private property leads us into contradictions.

To make land an object of huckstering—the land which is our one and all, the first condition of our existence—was the last step towards making oneself an object of huckstering. It was and is to this very day an immorality surpassed only by the immorality of self-alienation. And the original appropriation—the monopolisation of the land by a few, the exclusion of the rest from that which is the condition of their life— yields nothing in immorality to the subsequent huckstering of the land.

If here again we abandon private property, rent is reduced to its truth, to the rational notion which essentially lies at its root. The value of the land divorced from it as rent then reverts to the land itself. This value, to be measured by the productivity of equal areas of land subjected to equal applications of labour, is indeed taken into account as part of the production costs when determining the value of products; and like rent, it is the relation of productivity to competition—but to *true* competition, such as will be developed when its time comes.

We have seen that capital and labour are initially identical; we see further from the explanations of the economist himself that, in the process of production, capital, the result of labour, is immediately transformed again into the substratum, into the material of labour; and that therefore the momentarily postulated separation of capital from labour is immediately superseded by the unity of both. And yet the economist separates capital from labour, and yet clings to the division without giving any other recognition to their unity than by his definition of capital as "stored-up labour." The split between capital and labour resulting from private property is nothing but the inner dichotomy of labour corresponding to this divided condition and arising out of it. And after this separation is accomplished, capital is divided once more into the original capital and profit—the increment of capital, which it receives in the process of production; although in practice profit is immediately lumped together with capital and set into motion with it. Indeed, even profit is in its turn split into interest and profit proper. In the case of interest, the absurdity of these splits is carried to the extreme. The immorality of lending at interest, of receiving without working, merely for making a loan, though already implied in private property, is only too obvious, and has long ago been recognised for what it is by unprejudiced popular consciousness, which in such matters is usually right. All these subtle splits and divisions stem from the original separation of capital from labour and from the culmination of this separation—the division of mankind into capitalists and workers—a division which daily becomes ever more acute, and which, as we shall see, is *bound* to deepen. This separation, however, like the separation already considered of land from capital and labour, is in the final analysis an impossible separation. What share land, capital and labour each have in any particular product cannot be determined. The three magnitudes are incommensurable. The land produces the raw material, but not without capital and labour. Capital presupposes land and labour. And labour presupposes *at least* land, and usually also capital. The functions of these three elements are completely different, and are not to be measured by a fourth common standard. Therefore, when it comes to dividing the proceeds among the three elements under existing conditions, there is no inherent standard; it is an entirely alien and with regard to them fortuitous standard that decides—competition, the cunning right of the stronger. Rent implies competition; profit on capital is solely determined by competition; and the position with regard to wages we shall see presently.

If we abandon private property, then all these unnatural divisions disappear. The difference between interest and profit disappears; capital is nothing without labour, without movement. The significance of profit is reduced to the weight which capital carries in the determination of the costs of production, and profit thus remains inherent in capital, in the same way as capital itself reverts to its original unity with labour.

Labour—the main factor in production, the "source of wealth" free human activity—comes off badly with the economist. Just as capital has already been separated from labour, so labour is now in turn split for a second time: the product of labour confronts labour as wages, is separated from it, and is in its turn as usual determined by competition—there being, as we have seen, no firm standard determining labour's share in production. If we do away with private property, this unnatural separation also disappears. Labour becomes its own reward, and the true significance of the wages of labour, hitherto alienated, comes to light—namely, the significance of labour for the determination of the production costs of a thing.

We have seen that in the end everything comes down to competition, so long as private property exists. It is the economist's principal category—his most beloved daughter, whom he ceaselessly caresses—and look out for the Medusa's head which she will show you!

The immediate consequence of private property was the split of production into two opposing sides—the natural and the human sides, the soil which without fertilisation by man is dead and sterile, and human activity, the first condition of which is that very soil. Furthermore we have seen how human activity in its turn was dissolved into labour and capital, and how these two sides antagonistically confronted each other. Thus we already had the struggle of the three elements against one another, instead of their mutual support; now we have to add that private property brings in its wake the fragmentation of each of these elements. One piece of land stands confronted by another, one capital by another, one labourer by another. In other words, because private property isolates everyone in his own crude solitariness, and because, nevertheless, everyone has the same interest as his neighbour, one landowner stands antagonistically confronted by another, one capitalist by another, one worker by another. In this discord of identical interests resulting precisely from this identity is consummated the immorality of mankind's condition hitherto; and this consummation is competition.

The opposite of *competition is monopoly*. Monopoly was the war-cry of the Mercantilists; competition the battle-cry of the liberal economists. It is easy to see that this antithesis is again a quite hollow antithesis. Every competitor *cannot but* desire to have the monopoly, be he worker, capitalist or landowner. Each smaller group of competitors cannot but desire to have the monopoly for itself against all others. Competition is based on self-interest, and self-interest in turn breeds monopoly. In short, competition passes over into monopoly. On the other hand, monopoly cannot stem the tide of competition—indeed, it itself breeds competition; just as a prohibition of imports, for instance, or high tariffs positively breed the competition of smuggling. The contradiction of competition is exactly the same as that of private property. It is in the interest of each to possess everything, but in the interest of the whole that each possess an equal amount. Thus, the general and the individual interest are diametrically opposed to each other. The contradiction of competition is that each cannot but desire the monopoly, whilst the whole as such is bound to lose by monopoly and must therefore remove it. Moreover, competition already presupposes monopoly—namely, the monopoly of property (and here the hypocrisy of the liberals comes once more to light); and so long as the monopoly of property exists, for so long the possession of monopoly is equally justified—for monopoly, once it exists, is also property. What a pitiful half-measure, therefore, to attack the small monopolies, and to leave untouched the basic monopoly! And if we add to this the economist's proposition mentioned above, that nothing has value which cannot be monopolised—that nothing, therefore, which does not permit of such monopolisation can enter this arena of competition—then our assertion that competition presupposes monopoly is completely justified.

The law of competition is that demand and supply always strive to complement each other, and therefore never do so. The two sides are torn apart again and transformed into flat opposition. Supply always follows close on demand without ever quite covering it. It is either too big or too small, never corresponding to demand; because in this unconscious condition of mankind no one knows how big supply or demand is. If demand is greater than supply the price rises and, as a result, supply is to a certain degree stimulated. As soon as it comes on to the market, prices fall; and if it becomes greater than demand, then the fall in prices is so significant that demand is once again stimulated. So it goes on unendingly—a permanently unhealthy state of affairs—a constant alternation of over-stimulation and flagging which precludes all advance—a state of perpetual fluctuation without ever reaching its goal. This law with its constant adjustment, in which whatever is lost here is gained there, is regarded as something excellent by the economist. It is his chief glory—he cannot see enough of it, and considers it in all its possible and impossible applications. Yet it is obvious that this law is purely a law of nature and not a law of the mind. It is a law which produces revolution. The economist comes along with his lovely theory of demand and supply, proves to you that "one can never produce too much," and practice replies with trade crises, which reappear as regularly as the comets, and of which we have now on the average one every five to seven years. For the last eighty years these trade crises have arrived just as regularly as the great plagues did in the past—and they have brought in their train more misery and more immorality than the latter. (Compare Wade: *History of the Middle and Working Classes*, London, 1835, p. 211.) Of course, these commercial upheavals confirm the law, confirm it exhaustively—but in a manner different from that which the economist would have us believe to be the case. What are we to think of a law which can only assert itself through periodic upheavals? It is certainly a natural law based on the unconsciousness of the participants. If the producers as such knew how much the consumers required, if they were to organise production, if they were to share it out amongst themselves, then the fluctuations of competition and its tendency to crisis would be impossible. Carry on production consciously as human beings—not as dispersed atoms without consciousness of your species—and you have overcome all these artificial and untenable antitheses. But as long as you continue to produce in the present unconscious, thoughtless manner, at the mercy of chance—for just so long trade crises will remain; and each successive crisis is bound to become more universal and therefore worse than the preceding one; is bound to impoverish a larger body of small capitalists, and to augment in increasing proportion the numbers of the class who live by labour alone, thus considerably enlarging the mass of labour to be employed (the major problem of our economists) and finally causing a social revolution such as has never been dreamt of in the philosophy of the economists.

The perpetual fluctuation of prices such as is created by the condition of competition completely deprives trade of its last vestige of morality. It is no longer a question of *value;* the same system which appears to attach such importance to value, which confers on the abstraction of value in money form the honour of having an existence of its own— this very system destroys by means of competition the inherent value of all things, and daily and hourly changes the value-relationship of all things to one another. Where is there any possibility remaining in this whirlpool of an exchange based on a moral foundation? In this continuous up-and-down, everyone must seek to hit upon the most favourable moment for purchase and sale; everyone must become a speculator—that is to say, must reap where he has not sown; must enrich himself at the expense of others, must calculate on the misfortune of others, or let chance win for him. The speculator always counts on disasters, particularly on bad harvests. He utilises everything—for instance, the New York fire [December 16, 1835] in its time—and immorality's culminating point is the speculation on the Stock Exchange, where history, and with it mankind, is demoted to a means of gratifying the avarice of the calculating or gambling speculator. And let not the honest "respectable" merchant rise above the gambling on the Stock Exchange with a Pharisaic "I thank thee, O Lord...," etc. He is as bad as the speculators in stocks and shares. He speculates just as much as they do. He has to: competition compels him to. And his trading activity therefore implies the same immorality as theirs. The truth of the relation of competition is the relation of consumption to productivity. In a world worthy of mankind there will be no other competition than this. The community will have to calculate what it can produce with the means at its disposal; and in accordance with the relationship of this productive power to the mass of consumers it will determine how far it has to raise or lower production, how far it has to give way to, or curtail, luxury. But so that they may be able to pass a correct judgment on this relationship and on the increase in productive power to be expected from a rational state of affairs within the community, I invite my readers to consult the writings of the English Socialists, and partly also those of Fourier.

Subjective competition—the contest of capital against capital, of labour against labour, etc.—will under these conditions be reduced to the spirit of emulation grounded in human nature (a concept tolerably set forth so far only by Fourier), which after the transcendence of opposing interests will be confined to its proper and rational sphere.

The struggle of capital against capital, of labour against labour, of land against land, drives production to a fever-pitch at which production turns all natural and rational relations upside-down. No capital can stand the competition of another if it is not brought to the highest pitch of activity. No piece of land can be profitably cultivated if it does not continuously increase its productivity. No worker can hold his own against his competitors if he does not devote all his energy to labour. No one at all who enters into the struggle of competition can weather it without the utmost exertion of his energy, without renouncing every truly human purpose. The consequence of this over-exertion on the one side is, inevitably, slackening on the other. When the fluctuation of competition is small, when demand and supply, consumption and production, are almost equal, a stage must be reached in the development of production where there is so much superfluous productive power that the great mass of the nation has nothing to live on, that the people starve from sheer abundance. For some considerable time England has found herself in this crazy position, in this living absurdity. When production is subject to greater fluctuations, as it is bound to be in consequence of such a situation, then the alternation of boom and crisis, overproduction and slump, sets in. The economist has never been able to find an explanation for this mad situation. In order to explain it, he invented the population theory, which is just as senseless—indeed even more senseless than the contradiction of coexisting wealth and poverty. The economist *could not afford* to see the truth; he could not afford to admit that this contradiction is a simple consequence of competition; for in that case his entire system would have fallen to bits.

For us the matter is easy to explain. The productive power at mankind's disposal is immeasurable. The productivity of the soil can be increased *ad infinitum* by the application of capital, labour and science. According to the most able economists and statisticians (cf. Alison's *Principles of Population*, Vol. I, Chs. 1 and 2), "over-populated" Great Britain can be brought within ten years to produce a corn yield sufficient for a population six times its present size. Capital increases daily; labour power grows with population; and day by day science increasingly makes the forces of nature subject to man. This immeasurable productive capacity, handled consciously and in the interest of all, would soon reduce to a minimum the labour falling to the share of mankind. Left to competition, it does the same, but within a context of antitheses. One part of the land is cultivated in the best possible manner whilst another part—in Great Britain and Ireland thirty million acres of good land—lies barren. One part of capital circulates with colossal speed; another lies dead in the chest. One part of the workers works fourteen or sixteen hours a day, whilst another part stands idle and inactive, and starves. Or the partition leaves this realm of simultaneity: today trade is good; demand is very considerable; everyone works; capital is turned over with miraculous speed; farming flourishes; the workers work themselves sick. Tomorrow stagnation sets in. The cultivation of the land is not worth the effort; entire stretches of land remain untilled; the flow of capital suddenly freezes; the workers have no employment, and the whole country labours under surplus wealth and surplus population.

The economist cannot afford to accept this exposition of the subject as correct; otherwise, as has been said, he would have to give up his whole system of competition. He would have to recognise the hollowness of his antithesis of production and consumption, of surplus population and surplus wealth. To bring fact and theory into conformity with each other—since this fact simply could not be denied—the population theory was invented.

Malthus, the originator of this doctrine, maintains that population is always pressing on the means of subsistence; that as soon as production increases, population increases in the same proportion; and that the inherent tendency of the population to multiply in excess of the available means of subsistence is the root of all misery and all vice. For, when there are too many people, they have to be disposed of in one way or another: either they must be killed by violence or they must starve. But when this has happened, there is once more a gap which other multipliers of the population immediately start to fill up once more: and so the old misery begins all over again. What is more, this is the case in all circumstances—not only in civilized, but also in primitive conditions. In New Holland,[62] with a population density of *one* per square mile, the savages suffer just as much from over-population as England. In short, if we want to be consistent, we must admit *that the earth was already over-populated when only one man existed.* The implications of this line of thought are that since it is precisely the poor who are the surplus, nothing should be done for them except to make their dying of starvation as easy as possible, and to convince them that it cannot be helped and that there is no other salvation for their whole class than keeping propagation down to the absolute minimum. Or if this proves impossible, then it is after all better to establish a state institution for the painless killing of the children of the poor, such as "Marcus" has suggested, whereby each working-class family would be allowed to have two and a half children, any excess being painlessly killed. Charity is to be considered a crime, since it supports the augmentation of the surplus population. Indeed, it will be very advantageous to declare poverty a crime and to turn poor-houses into prisons, as has already happened in England as a result of the new "liberal" Poor Law. Admittedly it is true that this theory ill conforms with the Bible's doctrine of the perfection of God and of His creation; but "it is a poor refutation to enlist the Bible against facts."

Am I to go on any longer elaborating this vile, infamous theory, this hideous blasphemy against nature and mankind? Am I to pursue its consequences any further? Here at last we have the immorality of the economist brought to its highest pitch. What

---

[62] The old name for Australia.—Ed.

are all the wars and horrors of the monopoly system compared with this theory! And it is just this theory which is the keystone of the liberal system of free trade, whose fall entails the downfall of the entire edifice. For if here competition is proved to be the cause of misery, poverty and crime, who then will still dare to speak up for it?

In his above-mentioned work, Alison has shaken the Malthusian theory by bringing in the productive power of the land, and by opposing to the Malthusian principle the fact that each adult can produce more than he himself needs—a fact without which mankind could not multiply, indeed could not even exist; if it were not so how could those still growing up live? But Alison does not go to the root of the matter, and therefore in the end reaches the same conclusion as Malthus. True enough, he proves that Malthus' principle is incorrect, but cannot gainsay the facts which have impelled Malthus to his principle.

If Malthus had not considered the matter so one-sidedly, he could not have failed to see that surplus population or labour-power is invariably tied up with surplus wealth, surplus capital and surplus landed property. The population is only too large where the productive power as a whole is too large. The condition of every over-populated country, particularly England, since the time when Malthus wrote, makes this abundantly clear. These were the facts which Malthus ought to have considered in their totality, and whose consideration was bound to have led to the correct conclusion. Instead, he selected one fact, gave no consideration to the others, and therefore arrived at his crazy conclusion. The second error he committed was to confuse means of subsistence with [means of] employment. That population is always pressing on the means of employment—that the number of people produced depends on the number of people who can be employed—in short, that the production of labour-power has been regulated so far by the law of competition and is therefore also exposed to periodic crises and fluctuations—this is a fact whose establishment constitutes Malthus' merit. But the means of employment are not the means of subsistence. Only in their end-result are the means of employment increased by the increase in machin-epower and capital. The means of subsistence increase as soon as productive power increases even slightly. Here a new contradiction in economics comes to light. The economist's "demand" is not the real demand; his "consumption" is an artificial consumption. For the economist, only that person really demands, only that person is a real consumer, who has an equivalent to offer for what he receives. But if it is a fact that every adult produces more than he himself can consume, that children are like trees which give superabundant returns on the outlays invested in them—and these certainly are facts, are they not?—then it must be assumed that each worker ought to be able to produce far more than he needs and that the community, therefore, ought to be very glad to provide him with everything he needs; one must consider a large family to be a very welcome gift for the community. But the economist, with his crude outlook, knows no other equivalent than that which is paid to him in tangible ready cash. He is so firmly set in his antitheses that the most striking facts are of as little concern to him as the most scientific principles.

We destroy the contradiction simply by transcending it. With the fusion of the interests now opposed to each other there disappears the contradiction between excess population here and excess wealth there; there disappears the miraculous fact (more miraculous than all the miracles of all the religions put together) that a nation has to starve from sheer wealth and plenty; and there disappears the crazy assertion that the earth lacks the power to feed men. This assertion is the pinnacle of Christian economics—and that our economics is essentially Christian I could have proved from every proposition, from every category, and shall in fact do so in due course. The

Malthusian theory is but the economic expression of the religious dogma of the contradiction of spirit and nature and the resulting corruption of both. As regards religion, and together with religion, this contradiction was resolved long ago, and I hope that in the sphere of economics I have likewise demonstrated the utter emptiness of this contradiction. Moreover, I shall not accept as competent any defence of the Malthusian theory which does not explain to me on the basis of its own principles how a people can starve from sheer plenty and bring this into harmony with reason and fact.

At the same time, the Malthusian theory has certainly been a necessary point of transition which has taken us an immense step further. Thanks to this theory, as to economics as a whole, our attention has been drawn to the productive power of the earth and of mankind; and after overcoming this economic despair we have been made for ever secure against the fear of overpopulation. We derive from it the most powerful economic arguments for a social transformation. For even if Malthus were completely right, this transformation would have to be undertaken straight away; for only this transformation, only the education of the masses which it provides, makes possible that moral restraint of the propagative instinct which Malthus himself presents as the most effective and easiest remedy for overpopulation. Through this theory we have come to know the deepest degradation of mankind, their dependence on the conditions of competition. It has shown us how in the last instance private property has turned man into a commodity whose production and destruction also depend solely on demand; how the system of competition has thus slaughtered, and daily continues to slaughter, millions of men. All this we have seen, and all this drives us to the abolition of this degradation of mankind through the abolition of private property, competition and the opposing interests.

Yet, so as to deprive the universal fear of overpopulation of any possible basis, let us once more return to the relationship of productive power to population. Malthus establishes a formula on which he bases his entire system: population is said to increase in a geometrical progression—1+2+4+8+16+32, etc.; the productive power of the land in an arithmetical progression—1+2+3+4+5+6. The difference is obvious, is terrifying; but is it correct? Where has it been proved that the productivity of the land increases in an arithmetical progression? The extent of land is limited. All right! The labour-power to be employed on this land-surface increases with population. Even if we assume that the increase in yield due to increase in labour does not always rise in proportion to the labour, there still remains a third element which, admittedly, never means anything to the economist—science—whose progress is as unlimited and at least as rapid as that of population. What progress does the agriculture of this century owe to chemistry alone—indeed, to two men alone, Sir Humphry Davy and Justus Liebig! But science increases at least as much as population. The latter increases in proportion to the size of the previous generation, science advances in proportion to the knowledge bequeathed to it by the previous generation, and thus under the most ordinary conditions also in a geometrical progression. And what is impossible to science? But it is absurd to talk of over-population so long as "there is 'enough waste land in the valley of the Mississippi for the whole population of Europe to be transplanted there;"[63] so long as no more than one-third of the earth can be considered cultivated, and so long as the production of this third itself can be raised sixfold and more by the application of improvements already known.

---

[63] A. Alison, loc. cit., p. 548.—Ed.

Thus, competition sets capital against capital, labour against labour, landed property against landed property; and likewise each of these elements against the other two. In the struggle the stronger wins; and in order to predict the outcome of the struggle, we shall have to investigate the strength of the contestants. First of all, labour is weaker than either landed property or capital, for the worker must work to live, whilst the landowner can live on his rent, and the capitalist on his interest, or, if the need arises, on his capital or on capitalised property in land. The result is that only the very barest necessities, the mere means of subsistence, fall to the lot of labour; whilst the largest part of the products is shared between capital and landed property. Moreover, the stronger worker drives the weaker out of the market, just as larger capital drives out smaller capital, and larger landed property drives out smaller landed property. Practice confirms this conclusion. The advantages which the larger manufacturer and merchant enjoy over the smaller, and the big landowner over the owner of a single acre, are well known. The result is that already under ordinary conditions, in accordance with the law of the stronger, large capital and large landed property swallow small capital and small landed property—i.e., centralisation of property. In crises of trade and agriculture, this centralisation proceeds much more rapidly.

In general large property increases much more rapidly than small property, since a much smaller portion is deducted from its proceeds as property-expenses. This law of the centralisation of private property is as immanent in private property as all the others. The middle classes must increasingly disappear until the world is divided into millionaires and paupers, into large landowners and poor farm labourers. All the laws, all the dividing of landed property, all the possible splitting-up of capital, are of no avail: this result must and will come, unless it is anticipated by a total transformation of social conditions, a fusion of opposed interests, an abolition of private property.

Free competition, the keyword of our present-day economists, is an impossibility. Monopoly at least intended to protect the consumer against fraud, even if it could not in fact do so. The abolition of monopoly, however, opens the door wide to fraud. You say that competition carries with it the remedy for fraud, since no one will buy bad articles. But that means that everyone has to be an expert in every article, which is impossible. Hence the necessity for monopoly, which many articles in fact reveal. Pharmacies, etc., must have a monopoly. And the most important article—money—requires a monopoly most of all. Whenever the circulating medium has ceased to be a state monopoly it has invariably produced a trade crisis; and the English economists, Dr. Wade among them, do concede in this case the necessity for monopoly. But monopoly is no protection against counterfeit money. One can take one's stand on either side of the question: the one is as difficult as the other. Monopoly produces free competition, and the latter, in turn, produces monopoly. Therefore both must fall, and these difficulties must be resolved through the transcendence of the principle which gives rise to them.

Competition has penetrated all the relationships of our life and completed the reciprocal bondage in which men now hold themselves. Competition is the great mainspring which again and again jerks into activity our aging and withering social order, or rather disorder; but with each new exertion it also saps a part of this order's waning strength. Competition governs the numerical advance of mankind; it likewise governs its moral advance. Anyone who has any knowledge of the statistics of crime must have been struck by the peculiar regularity with which crime advances year by year, and with which certain causes produce certain crimes. The extension of the factory system is followed everywhere by an increase in crime. The number of arrests, of criminal cases—indeed, the number of murders, burglaries, petty thefts, etc., for a large town or for a district—can be predicted year by year with unfailing precision, as has been done often enough in England This regularity proves that crime, too, is governed by competition, that society creates a *demand* for crime which is met by a corresponding *supply;* that the gap created by the arrest, transportation or execution of a certain number is at once filled by others, just as every gap in population is at once filled by new arrivals; in other words, that crime presses on the means of punishment just as the people press on the means of employment. How just it is to punish criminals under these circumstances, quite apart from any other considerations, I leave to the judgment of my readers. Here I am merely concerned in demonstrating the extension of competition into the moral sphere, and in showing to what deep degradation private property has brought man.

In the struggle of capital and land against labour, the first two elements enjoy yet another special advantage over labour—the assistance of science; for in present conditions science, too, is directed against labour. Almost all mechanical inventions, for instance, have been occasioned by the lack of labour-power; in particular Hargreaves', Crompton's and Arkwright's cotton-spinning machines. There has never been an intense demand for labour which did not result in an invention that increased labour productivity considerably, thus diverting demand away from human labour. The history of England from 1770 until now is a continuous demonstration of this. The last great invention in cotton-spinning, the self-acting mule, was occasioned solely by the demand for labour, and rising wages. It doubled machine-labour, and thereby cut down hand-labour by half; it threw half the workers out of employment, and thereby reduced the wages of the others by half; it crushed a plot of the workers against the factory owners, and destroyed the last vestige of strength with which labour had still held out in the unequal struggle against capital. (Cf. Dr. Ure, *Philosophy of Manufactures, Vol. 2.*) The economist now says, however, that in its final result machinery is favourable to the workers, since it makes production cheaper and thereby creates a new and larger market for its products, and thus ultimately reemploys the workers put out of work. Quite right. But is the economist forgetting, then, that the production of labour-power is regulated by competition; that labour-power is always pressing on the means of employment, and that, therefore, when these advantages are due to become operative, a surplus of competitors for work is already waiting for them, and will thus render these advantages illusory; whilst the disadvantages—the sudden withdrawal of the means of subsistence from one half of the workers and the fall in wages for the other half—are not illusory? Is the economist forgetting that the progress of invention never stands still, and that these disadvantages, therefore, perpetuate themselves? Is he forgetting that with the division of labour, developed to such a high degree by our civilisation, a worker can only live if he can be used at this particular machine for this particular detailed operation; that the change-over from one type of employment to another, newer type is almost invariably an absolute impossibility for the adult worker?

In turning my attention to the effects of machinery, I am brought to another subject less directly relevant—the factory system; and I have neither the inclination nor the time to treat this here. Besides, I hope to have an early opportunity to expound in detail the despicable immorality of this system, and to expose mercilessly the economist's hypocrisy which here appears in all its brazenness.

THE END

CPSIA information can be obtained
at www.ICGtesting.com
Printed in the USA
LVOW12s1733210717

541992LV00001B/72/P